D1034002

Have you ever thoughtlessly sung a hymn, carried along by the familiar tune and well-known words, but disengaged in your heart and mind? In this intriguing volume, Leland Ryken is about to rescue you from such mindless, if melodic, repetition. By analyzing the poetry of forty well-known and beloved hymns, the author offers insight into these compositions as verse, enabling readers to appreciate the form and style of each piece. He also highlights the theology of each poem and links it to Scripture, providing ample material for meditation and prayer as well as inspiration for robust and thoughtful singing!

—**Rhett P. Dodson**, Senior Minister, Grace Presbyterian Church, Hudson, Ohio

A foundation of powerful and beautiful hymns is essential in the development of a community of believers and the expression of God's goodness through their lives. Thank you, Dr. Ryken, for this resource to the church.

—**Keith Getty**, Award-Winning Hymnwriter, Musician

What a great idea for a book! Professor Ryken helps hymn lovers to slow down and savor the words of such classic hymns as "Holy, Holy, Holy," "Amazing Grace," and "Come, Thou Fount of Every Blessing." While providing fascinating historical and authorial background, Ryken draws us into the special poetic language and metaphors that have made each hymn so beloved, memorable, and life-changing.

—**Louis Markos**, Professor in English and Scholar in Residence, Houston Baptist University; Author, *Literature: A Student's Guide* and *On the Shoulders of Hobbits: The Road to Virtue with Tolkein and Lewis*

This fine little book will serve as a salutary antidote to the thinning content of much of what passes for worship music today. Contemporary Christian music is in desperate need of theological depth.

Leland Ryken brings all of his poetic experience as a master teacher to bear on this critical subject. His poetic sensibilities have enabled him to make impeccable choices. I highly recommend this book as an aid to worship, an instruction in the value of poetry, and a vital voice in the contemporary conversation about worship music.

> —**Gregory Reynolds**, Editor, the *Ordained Servant* Journal; Pastor Emeritus; Author

The "lyric" of a song is a lyric *poem*. Sometimes the music draws all our attention, so that we skim over the words and what they mean. This is certainly true of hymns. Their lyrics are devotional poems of the highest order, and reading them closely can be a spiritual experience. Leland Ryken takes the texts of forty classic hymns and gives us just the help we need to understand their meaning and appreciate their greatness. In doing so, he helps Christians to realize why these time-honored hymns are such treasures.

> —**Gene Edward Veith**, Professor of Literature Emeritus, Patrick Henry College

If you are seeking God's will for your life and are faced with obstacles, if you are a student of poetry and desire fresh insights into literary devices, if you are a song writer like I am and you need some excellent worship texts, this short collection of hymn poems will strengthen your faith *and* your craft. I have read these poems and meditations for my daily devotions, and every day I found fresh insights from Watts, Cowper, or Francis Havergal. Though we usually sing these verses with fellow worshipers, they are rich food for contemplation.

> —**James Ward**, Recording Artist, Singer-Songwriter

In his fascinating study of poetry as praise, Leland Ryken breathes life into the old hymns and, by doing so, reminds us how to sing to the Lord a new song.

> —**Carolyn Weber**, Award-winning Author; Professor, University of Western Ontario, and Heritage College and Seminary

40
Favorite
Hymns
on the
Christian Life

40
Favorite
Hymns
on the
Christian Life

A CLOSER LOOK
AT THEIR SPIRITUAL
AND POETIC MEANING

LELAND RYKEN

P&R
P U B L I S H I N G
P.O. BOX 817 • PHILLIPSBURG • NEW JERSEY 08865-0817

© 2019 by Leland Ryken

All rights reserved. No part of this book may be reproduced, stored in a retrieval system, or transmitted in any form or by any means—electronic, mechanical, photocopy, recording, or otherwise—except for brief quotations for the purpose of review or comment, without the prior permission of the publisher, P&R Publishing Company, P.O. Box 817, Phillipsburg, New Jersey 08865-0817.

Unless otherwise indicated, Scripture quotations are from the ESV® Bible (The Holy Bible, English Standard Version®), copyright © 2001 by Crossway, a publishing ministry of Good News Publishers. Used by permission. All rights reserved.

Scripture quotations marked (KJV) are taken from the King James Version.

Italics within Scripture quotations indicate emphasis added.

Permission to reprint the following three hymns is hereby gratefully acknowledged:

"Tell Out, My Soul." Words: Timothy Dudley-Smith. © 1962, Ren. 1990 Hope Publishing Company, Carol Stream, IL 60188. All rights reserved. Used by permission.

"How Great Thou Art." Words: Stuart K. Hine. Music: Swedish folk melody/adapt. and arr. Stuart K. Hine. © 1949, 1953 The Stuart Hine Trust CIO. All rights in the USA its territories and possessions, except print rights, administered by Capitol CMG Publishing. USA, North and Central American print rights and all Canadian and South American rights administered by Hope Publishing Company. All other North and Central American rights administered by The Stuart Hine Trust CIO. Rest of the world rights administered by Integrity Music Europe. All rights reserved. Used by permission.

"In Christ Alone." Writers: Keith Getty and Stuart Townend. Copyright © 2002 Thankyou Music (PRS) (adm. Worldwide at CapitolCMGPublishing.com excluding Europe which is adm. by Integrity Music, part of the David C. Cook family. Songs@integrity music.com) All rights reserved. Used by permission.

All other hymn texts reprinted in this anthology are in the public domain.

Printed in the United States of America

Library of Congress Cataloging-in-Publication Data

Names: Ryken, Leland, author.
Title: 40 favorite hymns on the Christian life : a closer look at their spiritual and
  poetic meaning / Leland Ryken.
Other titles: Forty favorite hymns on the Christian life
Description: Phillipsburg : P&R Publishing, 2019. | Includes bibliographical references.
Identifiers: LCCN 2018043560| ISBN 9781629956176 (hardcover) | ISBN
  9781629956183 (epub) | ISBN 9781629956190 (mobi)
Subjects: LCSH: Hymns--History and criticism. | Christian life--Miscellanea.
Classification: LCC BV310 .R95 2019 | DDC 264/.23--dc23
LC record available at https://lccn.loc.gov/2018043560

For Nancy and Jeremy

Contents

Introduction   11

Holy, Holy, Holy   15
Reginald Heber

O for a Thousand Tongues to Sing   18
Charles Wesley

Amazing Grace   21
John Newton

Fairest Lord Jesus   24
Author Unknown

Jesus, Thou Joy of Loving Hearts   27
Bernard of Clairvaux

The Church's One Foundation   30
Samuel John Stone

Come, We That Love the Lord   34
Isaac Watts

Just as I Am   37
Charlotte Elliott

And Can It Be?   40
Charles Wesley

How Firm a Foundation 44
Author Unknown

Crown Him with Many Crowns 47
Matthew Bridges; Godfrey Thring

All Hail the Power of Jesus' Name 51
Edward Perronet

O Worship the King 54
Sir Robert Grant

Come, Thou Fount of Every Blessing 57
Robert Robinson

Love Divine, All Loves Excelling 61
Charles Wesley

Like a River Glorious 64
Frances Ridley Havergal

In Christ Alone 68
Keith Getty and Stuart Townend

Rock of Ages 71
Augustus Toplady

How Great Thou Art 74
Stuart K. Hine

It Is Well with My Soul 78
Horatio Spafford

Abide with Me 81
Henry Lyte

Ye Holy Angels Bright 84
Richard Baxter

A Mighty Fortress Is Our God   88
Martin Luther

Come, Thou Almighty King   92
Author Unknown

Tell Out, My Soul   95
Timothy Dudley-Smith

Guide Me, O Thou Great Jehovah   98
William Williams

Be Thou My Vision   101
Author Unknown

A Shelter in the Time of Storm   104
Vernon J. Charlesworth

Glorious Things of Thee Are Spoken   107
John Newton

Jesus Shall Reign   111
Isaac Watts

My Hope Is Built on Nothing Less   114
Edward Mote

Savior, Like a Shepherd Lead Us   117
Dorothy Thrupp

Take My Life, and Let It Be   121
Frances Ridley Havergal

May the Mind of Christ My Savior   124
Kate B. Wilkinson

To God Be the Glory   127
Fanny J. Crosby

Christ Is Made the Sure Foundation   130
  John M. Neale

God Moves in a Mysterious Way   134
  William Cowper

Fill Thou My Life, O Lord My God   137
  Horatius Bonar

Jesus, the Very Thought of Thee   140
  Bernard of Clairvaux

Praise to the Lord, the Almighty   143
  Joachim Neander

Conclusion   147
Notes   149
Glossary of Literary Terms   153

Introduction

I T will doubtless surprise most readers to learn that until 1870, the customary format of a hymnal was a small (five-by-three-inch) book consisting of words only. The most accurate designation for such a book is an "anthology of devotional poems." These anthologies were carried back and forth between home and office and school and church. *Forty Favorite Hymns on the Christian Life* seeks to revive this tradition of experiencing familiar hymns as poems.

Among several good reasons for such a revival is the fact that every hymn is a poem first, and only later becomes a hymn. As a verbal text, a hymn possesses all the qualities of a poem. Only when it is paired with music does it become a hymn. Much is gained by the singing of hymns accompanied by music, but much is also lost.

This anthology of hymnic poems aims to restore what has been lost. An immediate gain comes from reading the successive stanzas in linear fashion, with one stanza following its predecessor. Our gaze keeps moving forward instead of returning to the same starting point at the beginning of each stanza. The result is a clear sense of the sequential progression of thought and feeling, as it grows organically from beginning to end.

A second advantage of reading a hymn as a poem is that we can read slowly instead of being hurried along by the music and singing. Poetry is concentrated, and it accordingly requires pondering and analyzing. When reading a poem, we can take as long as the text requires. Such contemplative reading allows us to pause on individual images, letting the literal picture register in our imagination and then noting the connotations and emotions that flow from each image. Figures of speech such as metaphors and similes likewise ask to have their meanings unpacked.

Much of the beauty that we experience when we sing hymns is the beauty of the music. Experiencing hymns as poems puts the focus on the verbal beauty of the words and phrases. The great hymns of Christian tradition are an untapped source of devotional poetry, just waiting to be made available for the pleasure and edification of Christians.

It is not an overstatement to claim that this anthology of hymns presented and analyzed as devotional poems will introduce readers to the hymns they never knew. Readers will realize that they have been deprived of a treasure that was never opened to them.

Every entry in this anthology consists of three elements—a hymnic poem, an explication of the poem, and a passage from the Bible that ties into the hymn and its explication. The Bible passages are intended to enhance the reading of this book for devotional purposes.

T HE explications of the poems should be used as a lens through which to look closely at the accompanying texts. They are not a substitute for the poems, nor are they detachable pieces of information. They function as a travel guide at a site, interpreting what the travelers are looking at and bringing out features that would otherwise be missed. There is no prescribed order for reading a poem and its accompanying explication, but regardless of whether you read the poem or the explication first, the explication is designed to send you back to the text repeatedly. For example, every explication includes an account of the flow of the successive stanzas or sections of the poem under consideration and examines how different rhetorical and literary techniques are used in each one. Thus, if the explication says something about image patterns or allusions, that insight comes to fruition only if you go back to the text and see how the statement in the explication is true. This book will achieve its intended purpose only if you go back and forth between a poem and its accompanying explication.

A glossary at the back of the book gives definitions for the poetic and literary terms that will be used in the discussions of the different poems.

Holy, Holy, Holy

Reginald Heber (1783–1826)

Holy, holy, holy, Lord God Almighty!
Early in the morning our song shall rise to thee.
Holy, holy, holy! Merciful and mighty,
God in three persons, blessed Trinity!

Holy, holy, holy! All the saints adore thee,
Casting down their golden crowns around the glassy sea;
Cherubim and seraphim falling down before thee,
Who wert and art and evermore shalt be.

Holy, holy, holy! Though the darkness hide thee,
Though the eye of sinful man thy glory may not see,
Only thou art holy; there is none beside thee,
Perfect in power, in love, and purity.

Holy, holy, holy! Lord God Almighty!
All thy works shall praise thy name, in earth and sky and sea.
Holy, holy, holy! Merciful and mighty,
God in three persons, blessed Trinity!

T HE importance of this hymn, which was first published
in 1826, is suggested by the fact it belongs to a very elite

circle of hymns that are included in nearly every English-language hymnbook. It was well regarded in its own day, as well—the Victorian poet Alfred, Lord Tennyson is well attested to have admired this hymn in particular.

The high style of the poem is its most obvious formal quality. Among the features of this high style are exalted epithets for God and the piling up of adjectives, nouns, and verbs in patterns of two and three, creating an effect of irrepressible energy. An example is "perfect in power, in love, and purity." The dominant tone is exaltation. This exuberance is enhanced by the length of the lines, which are nearly twice as long as what we find in most hymns. Despite this grandeur, there is a single rhyming sound (the long *e*) for the entire poem.

Multiple genres converge in this exalted poem. Despite its brevity, the poem can be called an *ode*, which handbooks define as an exalted poem on a dignified subject written in the high style. Most odes praise their subject, and this poem fits the pattern, thereby also qualifying as a psalm of praise. Because the speaker in the poem addresses God directly, the poem is also a prayer. And since the opening line is an English translation of a line from ancient church liturgy, the adjective *liturgical* is an accurate one to attach to the poem. In this vein, we might note that Reginald Heber, an Anglican clergyman, composed the hymn for Trinity Sunday.

Because of the conspicuous repetition of the word *holy*, it would be easy to conclude that God's holiness is the theme of the poem, but that would be misleading. The ascription of holiness to God is part of the more general theme of the worthiness of God's character. Other aspects of Gods worthiness are also praised. Under the unifying umbrella of God's worthiness of praise, the poet constructs a mosaic of specific variations on the central theme: God's holiness, God's existence as a Trinity, the attributes of God (with mercy, might, glory, power, love, and purity all mentioned), the universality with which God is extolled (by people in stanza 1, by saints and angels in stanza 2, and by the creatures of nature in stanza 4). Stanza 3 is a kind of "aside" in which the poet pauses to note that human sinfulness has a way of obscuring people's ability to perceive God's glory.

The triumph of this poem is that it sweeps us up and makes us participants in the very praise that, according to the poem, the universe is already ascribing to God on earth and in heaven.

I T is nearly certain that the poet composed this exalted hymn of praise with Revelation 4:8, 10–11 serving as his model:

The four living creatures . . . never cease to say,

"Holy, holy, holy, is the Lord God Almighty . . . !"

. . . The twenty-four elders fall down before him who is seated on the throne and worship him who lives forever and ever. They cast their crowns before the throne, saying,

"Worthy are you, our Lord and God,
to receive glory and honor and power."

O for a Thousand Tongues to Sing

Charles Wesley (1707–1788)

O for a thousand tongues to sing
My great Redeemer's praise,
The glories of my God and king,
The triumphs of his grace.

My gracious master and my God,
Assist me to proclaim,
To spread through all the earth abroad,
The honors of thy name.

Jesus! the name that charms our fears,
That bids our sorrows cease;
'Tis music in the sinner's ears,
'Tis life and health and peace.

He breaks the power of canceled sin,
He sets the prisoner free;
His blood can make the foulest clean;
His blood availed for me.

He speaks, and listening to his voice,
New life the dead receive;

The mournful, broken hearts rejoice,
The humble poor believe.

Hear him, ye deaf; his praise, ye dumb,
Your loosened tongues employ;
Ye blind, behold your Savior come,
And leap, ye lame, for joy.

F OR people who know this hymn only in its familiar form as printed above, the original context holds some surprises. Written by one of the founders of English Methodism, the first published version of this hymn in 1740 bore the title "For the Anniversary Day of One's Conversion." The explanation is that Wesley composed the hymn a year after his conversion, intending it as a testimony to God's salvation of his soul. Although there is certainly an element of universal praise in the poem, we should also assimilate it as an individual's thanksgiving to God for personal salvation.

An even bigger surprise is that the original hymn consisted of eighteen stanzas! Furthermore, the familiar opening stanza was not the first verse but the seventh. In the original version, the first stanza is a doxology addressed to God, followed by five autobiographical stanzas that recount the author's conversion and coming into full assurance of salvation. Then the hymn turns from testimony to praise with the familiar line, "O for a thousand tongues to sing."

The first two stanzas here are a lead-in to proclamation of God's glory. First the poet expresses a wish that he could adequately praise the triumphs of God's grace. Then, in stanza 2, he prays to God to assist him to proclaim the honors of the divine name. The unifying theme of these two stanzas is the poet's longing to proclaim God's praise adequately. The opening stanza draws upon a technique known as the inexpressibility motif, as the hyperbolic wish for a thousand tongues implicitly acknowledges that a solitary human cannot express God's glory adequately.

With the lead-in complete, the next three stanzas perform the wished-for and prayed-for proclamation of praise for the works of Jesus in redemption. The technique is the standard one in the poetry of praise—namely, the list or catalog of praiseworthy actions. If we look closely, we can find the following division of duties across the successive stanzas: the ability of Jesus to calm the human spirit and bring life and peace to it; the power of the blood of Jesus to cleanse from sin and guilt; the revival and rejoicing that follow forgiveness of sin. The stanzas are an anatomy of what conversion of soul brings to a person.

Following the proclamation of the acts of Jesus in his work of salvation, the poem moves in the final stanza to exhortation. Specifically, the company of the redeemed is called to rouse itself to participate in a grand celebration. Various groups are addressed by means of a technique known as apostrophe: direct address to someone not literally present—a standard way of expressing strong feeling.

The dominant feature of the poem is its tone of exuberance. From the opening wish for a thousand tongues to the concluding picture of leaping for joy, this signature hymn of Methodism uses familiar biblical imagery and vocabulary to send the human spirit soaring.

T HE catalog of Christ's saving acts in this hymn draws upon prophetic and gospel passages about the work of the Messiah. One of these is Luke 4:17–19:

> And the scroll of the prophet Isaiah was given to him [Jesus].
> He unrolled the scroll and found the place where it was written,

"The Spirit of the Lord is upon me,
    because he has anointed me
    to proclaim good news to the poor.
He has sent me to proclaim liberty to the captives
    and recovering of sight to the blind,
    to set at liberty those who are oppressed,
to proclaim the year of the Lord's favor."

Amazing Grace

John Newton (1725–1807)

Amazing grace! how sweet the sound,
That saved a wretch like me!
I once was lost but now am found,
Was blind but now I see.

'Twas grace that taught my heart to fear,
And grace my fears relieved;
How precious did that grace appear
The hour I first believed!

The Lord has promised good to me,
His word my hope secures;

He will my shield and portion be
As long as life endures.

Through many dangers, toils, and snares,
I have already come;
'Tis grace hath brought me safe thus far,
And grace will lead me home.

Yea, when this flesh and heart shall fail,
And mortal life shall cease,
I shall possess, within the veil,
A life of joy and peace.

When we've been there ten thousand years,
Bright shining as the sun,
We've no less days to sing God's praise
Than when we've first begun.

T HIS is the world's most famous hymn, sung around the world in many languages. In fact, a biographer claims that the hymn is sung publicly ten million times annually. Behind the hymn stands the biography of a great sinner (in the mode of Augustine's *Confessions*). John Newton had been a profane seaman and a slave trader. He was converted during a storm at sea that threatened his life. This life story of extraordinary sinfulness that required extraordinary grace for salvation is the autobiographical foundation on which the poem is constructed. But the fact that so many people resonate with it is testimony that it is every believer's story, not just Newton's.

At the level of imagery, the poem is built around a great contrast that puts two worlds on a collision course. One is a world of sin and fallenness—not just spiritually in a sinner's personal life, but in the whole earthly order. The vocabulary continually keeps this world of decay and misery alive in our awareness, with words like *wretch, lost, blind, dangers, toils, snares, fail, cease, dissolve like snow,* and *refuse to shine.* Set over against this lower world of unideal experience is an upper world of ideal experience, portrayed with words like *grace, found, good, hope, shield and portion, joy and peace, shining as the sun.* The poem thus roots us in the fallen earthly order but promises us the best that can be imagined. It is a song of hope, comfort, and confidence, with misery functioning as a foil to heighten the vision of bliss.

When we turn from this "global" view of the poem as a whole and look more closely at its parts, we find that each stanza has its own theme and, further, that the successive stanzas take us from the moment of conversion to eternity in heaven. The poem truly covers the totality of the spiritual life. The successive topics and experiences are as follows: personal conversion to salvation, with emphasis on celebrating this new condition; again a recounting of conversion, but this time with a retrospective look at the conviction of sin that led to belief; confidence in God's protection during earthly life; a look backward on life's difficulties and forward toward release from them; expression of hope for eternal joy and peace; and celebration of the eternal nature of life in heaven. With a little streamlining, we can see an arrangement by pairs of verses that cover past, present, and future.

Is there a poetic explanation for the fact that this has become the signature hymn of the English-speaking world? No; a benediction has fallen on it that cannot be fully explained. We can say, however, that the poem promises what we long for at the deepest level of our being: grace, salvation, going home, being safe within a heavenly veil, eternity in God's presence.

ALTHOUGH this poem does not keep its focus strictly on the grace named in the famous opening, that line is so captivating that we assimilate the whole poem as celebrating the triumphs of God's grace in our lives. Titus 2:11–13 is a good parallel passage, which unfolds as the poem does from past to future:

> For the grace of God has appeared, bringing salvation for all people, training us to renounce ungodliness and worldly passions, and to live self-controlled, upright, and godly lives in the present age, waiting for our blessed hope, the appearing of the glory of our great God and Savior Jesus Christ.

Fairest Lord Jesus

Author Unknown (seventeenth century)

Fairest Lord Jesus, ruler of all nature,
O Thou of God and man the Son,
Thee will I cherish, thee will I honor,
Thou my soul's glory, joy, and crown.

Fair are the meadows, fairer still the woodlands,
Robed in the blooming garb of spring:

Jesus is fairer, Jesus is purer,
Who makes the woeful heart to sing.

Fair is the sunshine, fairer still the moonlight,
And all the twinkling starry host:
Jesus shines brighter, Jesus shines purer
Than all the angels heaven can boast.

Beautiful Savior! Lord of the nations!
Son of God and Son of Man!
Glory and honor, praise, adoration,
Now and for evermore be thine.

T HIS is such a familiar English hymn that it comes as a surprise to learn how many mysteries surround it—beginning with the most basic questions about its true origins. A long tradition has labeled it "the crusaders' hymn," and romanticized nineteenth-century accounts pictured medieval crusaders and pilgrims singing it as they marched to Jerusalem. It is perhaps a small disappointment to learn that this legend cannot possibly be true. The earliest known version of the hymn dates from the latter part of the seventeenth century (1677). Other theories have put forth such contradictory sources as a Roman Catholic chant or a German folk hymn, and it has been ascribed elsewhere to the followers of early Reformer John Hus. There is disagreement about other features of the poem, too—even including who the translator is. The first and last stanzas of the hymn as commonly printed (and as printed above), in fact, are different English translations of the same German original.

When we turn to the actual text, things immediately become clearer and simpler. In fact, the hymn is often viewed and used as a children's hymn. Nature imagery figures prominently in the poem, and the appeal of nature is universal. Whereas many hymns take us on an excursion through multiple ideas and motifs, this poem keeps the focus single-mindedly on the superior beauty and attractiveness of Jesus (a strategy that literary scholars label "the superiority motif").

Offsetting this simplicity are pleasing elements of complexity. The poet imitates the biblical verse form known as parallelism, in which similar content is expressed two or three times consecutively in different words or images but in similar grammatical form. For example, "Thee will I cherish, Thee will I honor." As an extension of that, series of nouns pour out: "glory, joy, and crown." The opening and closing stanzas feature evocative epithets for Jesus: "Beautiful Savior! Lord of the nations!"

The use of nature in the middle two stanzas draws upon very old poetic traditions. Through the centuries, nature has provided a language for talking about various subjects. In love poetry and devotional poetry, for example, poets commonly evoke our sense of the beauty of nature and then transmute that sentiment for nature into feeling toward a romantic beloved or toward God. A common strategy, then, is to take this a step further—to compare the beloved to nature to the *detriment* of the latter, as the beloved is said to be better or more beautiful than nature. This is exactly what the writer of this poem does: he compares Jesus to the "best of the best" in nature, only to declare Jesus better.

This poem has a winning simplicity in its A-B-A envelope structure. The middle two stanzas elaborate the theme of Jesus' superiority by comparing him to nature. The opening and closing stanzas are bookends, highlighted by their being translations of the same German text. Instead of experiencing them as competing translations, we can view them as pleasing complements, enriching our experience of the original text.

T HE attraction of people to the beauty of Jesus' character and actions is a continuous thread throughout the gospel accounts of his life. The welcome that the Samaritans extended to Jesus, as recorded in John 4:40–42, is one such picture of how people were attracted to the beauty of Jesus as their Savior:

> So when the Samaritans came to him, they asked him to stay with them, and he stayed there two days. And many more believed because of his word. They said to the woman, "It is no longer because of what you said that we believe, for we have heard for ourselves, and we know that this is indeed the Savior of the world."

A line from this hymn summarizes that picture perfectly:

> Beautiful Savior! Lord of the nations!

Jesus, Thou Joy of Loving Hearts

Bernard of Clairvaux (1090–1153)

Jesus, thou joy of loving hearts,
Thou fount of life, thou light of men,
From the best bliss that earth imparts,
We turn unfilled to thee again.

Thy truth unchanged hath ever stood;
Thou savest those that on thee call;
To them that seek thee thou art good,
To them that find thee, all in all.

We taste thee, O thou living bread,
And long to feast upon thee still;
We drink of thee, the fountainhead,
And thirst our souls from thee to fill.

Our restless spirits yearn for thee,
Wherever our changeful lot is cast;
Glad when thy gracious smile we see,
Blessed when our faith can hold thee fast.

O Jesus, ever with us stay,
Make all our moments calm and bright;
Chase the dark night of sin away,
Shed over the world thy holy light.

B Y the time the French abbot Bernard penned this poem (here translated by Ray Palmer in 1858) in his monastery in the twelfth century, Augustine of Hippo's famous aphorism from the opening paragraph of his *Confessions* was eight hundred years old. That aphorism states that "our souls are restless till they rest in you" (meaning God). Perhaps with this famous saying echoing in his memory, Bernard composed an entire poem on the theme of the restless soul that finds its rest in Jesus. Like Augustine, Bernard addresses his reflections directly to Jesus.

Both of the unifying motifs—the restless soul and rest in Jesus—can be found in each of the five stanzas. In each stanza we can find an assertion, either stated or implied, that the human soul finds something about earthly life that renders it unsatisfying apart from Jesus. A second motif that we can uncover in each stanza is an acknowledgment that Jesus is the only satisfaction for human longing. One of the functions of poetry is to awaken longing; this famous poem arouses our longing for Jesus.

Another poetic strength of this composition is its format. The poem has a dramatic structure in which the speaker addresses Jesus from start to finish, making the poem a prayer. The speaker continuously casts himself on Jesus, and the reader is swept into a similar motion of the soul.

Within this format of a prayerful address to Jesus, the poem follows a firm sequential structure. The first four stanzas declare who Jesus is and praise him for being the satisfaction of human longing. These four stanzas each cover similar territory and thus have a repetitive structure. In the final stanza, the speaker moves from description to petition, lending a note of closure and finality.

Three qualities of the vocabulary and imagery contribute to the power of this poem. The poet uses an evocative vocabulary that awakens feeling with such words as *loving, best, good, all in all, long, thirst, fill, yearn, glad, blessed, calm, bright,* and *holy.* A second source of power is the presence of great archetypes of literature and life: fount, light, bread, drink, holding fast, and night. A third triumph of the poem is its exalted epithets or titles for Jesus: *joy of loving hearts, fount of life, light of men, living bread, the fountainhead.*

Ralph Waldo Emerson claimed that poets are *sayers*, sent into the world to express what the human race wants to be said but lacks the ability to say adequately. In this poem, Bernard becomes the spokesman for all believing souls—and on the issue that matters most.

T HIS hymn speaks of turning to Jesus as the only satisfaction of human longing. A famous statement uttered by Peter expresses the same thought:

> Simon Peter answered him [Jesus], "Lord, to whom shall we go [but unto you]? You have the words of eternal life, and we have believed, and have come to know, that you are the Holy One of God." (John 6:68–69)

The Church's One Foundation

Samuel John Stone (1839–1900)

The church's one foundation
Is Jesus Christ her Lord;
She is his new creation
By water and the Word:
From heaven he came and sought her
To be his holy bride;
With his own blood he bought her,
And for her life he died.

Elect from every nation,
Yet one o'er all the earth,
Her charter of salvation

One Lord, one faith, one birth;
One holy Name she blesses,
Partakes one holy food.
And to one hope she presses,
With every grace endued.

Though with a scornful wonder
Men see her sore oppressed,
By schisms rent asunder,
By heresies distressed,
Yet saints their watch are keeping,
Their cry goes up, "How long?"
And soon the night of weeping
Shall be the morn of song.

The church shall never perish!
Her dear Lord to defend,
To guide, sustain and cherish
Is with her to the end;
Though there be those that hate her,
And false sons in her pale,
Against or foe or traitor
She ever shall prevail.

'Mid toil and tribulation,
And tumult of her war,
She waits the consummation
Of peace for evermore;
Till with the vision glorious
Her longing eyes are blest,
And the great church victorious
Shall be the church at rest.

Yet she on earth hath union
With God the Three in One,
And mystic sweet communion
With those whose rest is won:
O happy ones and holy!
Lord, give us grace that we,
Like them, the meek and lowly,
On high may dwell with thee.

I F we look at this poem as a self-contained text without plac-
ing it in the context of its composition, we can see its essential
feature: namely, that it is a prolonged meditation on the nature
of the church. A stanza-by-stanza breakdown of the poem with
this central topic in view yields the following: the point that
Jesus is the foundation on which the church is built; a declaration of the unity of the church (with the word *one* appearing
eight times); an acknowledgment of threats to the unity of the
church; the confident assertion that the church will survive; a
longing to join the church triumphant in the eschaton; and an
assurance of the comfort derived by the church on earth from its
union with saints who have gone to heaven.

All of that is open to close reading of the text by itself, but
the topics that the poet chose for inclusion in his meditation
fall into place more clearly if we know the context within which
the poem was composed. Samuel John Stone was an Anglican
minister from an educationally privileged background who
began his lifetime of clerical service in London at a church
located in an underprivileged suburb. While there, Stone composed a collection of twelve hymns based on the individual
planks of the Apostles' Creed for the benefit of his theologically
ignorant parishioners. "The Church's One Foundation" is based
on statements in the creed about the holy catholic church and

the communion of saints, which explains the format of focused meditation on the nature of the church.

A further context explains the heavy emphasis on the church being beset with conflict. A few years before the composition of this hymnic poem, the Anglican church worldwide had been deeply divided over inroads of liberal views of the Bible that had originated in South Africa. Stone was a conservative in the battle. This context of denominational conflict helps to explain the consistent motif of battle in the poem, as the extravagant claims made about the triumph of the church are set against descriptions of circumstances that challenge such confidence. More specific contrasts also lend energy to the poem: diversity vs. unity, threat vs. security, now vs. then (i.e., the consummation in eternity), turmoil vs. rest and calm. A certain balance between realism and idealism emerges and begets confidence that the praise of the true church is not facile (glibly asserted).

Even when we sing it as a hymn, but even more so when we take time to ponder its images and phrases, the exultant eloquence of this poem stands out. One avenue toward assimilating this text as a poem is to relish its aphoristic turns of phrase and memorable images. Then as we continue to ponder the poetic texture, it becomes obvious that the poem is a collage of biblical allusions.

A website called *Congregational Singing* prints this hymn with nearly fifty wide-ranging biblical passages listed in an accompanying column, confirming that it is not based on a single passage from the Bible. Although the unity of the church is celebrated primarily in the second stanza, the spirit of Ephesians 4:4–6 breathes through the entire poem:

> There is one body and one Spirit—just as you were called to the one hope that belongs to your call—one Lord, one faith, one

baptism, one God and Father of all, who is over all and through all and in all.

Come, We That Love the Lord

Isaac Watts (1674–1748)

Come, we that love the Lord,
And let our joys be known;
Join in a song with sweet accord,
And thus surround the throne.

Let those refuse to sing
That never knew our God;
But children of the heavenly King
May speak their joys abroad.

The men of grace have found
Glory begun below;
Celestial fruits on earthly ground
From faith and hope may grow.

The hill of Zion yields
A thousand sacred sweets,

Before we reach the heavenly fields,
Or walk the golden streets.

Then let our songs abound,
And every tear be dry;
We're marching through Immanuel's ground
To fairer worlds on high.

Refrain
We're marching to Zion,
Beautiful, beautiful Zion;
We're marching upward to Zion,
The beautiful city of God.

W RITTEN by the "father of English hymnody," this
hymnic poem is also known by the title "We're Marching to Zion," on the strength of a refrain added by American
composer Robert Lowry more than half a century after Watts's
composition. This poem about the joys of heaven has affinities
with the genres of the elegiac poem and the funeral sermon.
Elegies move from a lament over the death of a specific person to consolation, which for Christian poets consists of an
awareness of the continuing life of the deceased in heaven.
Similarly, an expected part of a funeral sermon is that it offers
the heavenly existence of the deceased as a reason for the sorrowing survivors to be consoled. Congregants leave a funeral
service newly convicted that they should live in an awareness
of their heavenly destiny. "Come, We That Love the Lord" is
built around these motifs of our heavenly destination and the
effect it should have on us now. Additionally, the final stanza
incorporates the elegiac convention of dismissal of tears ("let
. . . every tear be dry").

If we look at the sequential unfolding of this poem, we see the following progression: The opening invitation (or command) to "come" is a summons to believers (i.e., "we that love the Lord") to sing about their joys. The effect is similar to opening a church door and inviting worshipers to enter. The second stanza continues the motif of encouraging believers to join a spiritual celebration, in a context that acknowledges that unbelievers lack the prerequisite that would enable them to participate (they "never knew our God"). The effect of this stanza is to tell us not to be deterred from worship by people who do not understand its appeal.

With the summons to sing complete, the remaining three stanzas become more specific and provide the content for the song we have been invited to sing. Stanzas 3 and 4 assert that heavenly joy can be experienced during our earthly lives. The fifth stanza, beginning with the causal word *then*, draws a conclusion based on what has been asserted—namely, that we should not sorrow, inasmuch as we are headed for a transcendent realm. The refrain clinches this optimistic point by sweeping us into a victory march.

There are three avenues by which we can claim the edification that this poem stands ready to offer. First, this is a poem of comfort and consolation in which the prospect of heaven obliterates every loss or sorrow that might otherwise drag us down. Second, the rapturous language used for heaven (e.g., "the heavenly fields," "the golden streets," "the beautiful city of God") makes this poem a triumph of the rhetoric of transcendence—one that fires our imaginations with the heavenly world above. Third, there is also a rhetoric of exhortation and persuasion at work, which implicitly exhorts us to make sure that the spiritual qualities of heavenly life are a reality in our lives right now.

T HE heartbeat of this poem is its pictures of the transcendent heavenly realm. The greatest biblical model for the Celestial City is the book of Revelation, with its descriptions such as the following:

> And he carried me away in the Spirit to a great, high mountain, and showed me the holy city Jerusalem coming down out of heaven from God, having the glory of God, its radiance like a most rare jewel, like a jasper, clear as crystal. . . .
>
> And the twelve gates were twelve pearls, each of the gates made of a single pearl, and the street of the city was pure gold, like transparent glass. (Rev. 21:10–11, 21)

Just as I Am

Charlotte Elliott (1789–1871)

Just as I am, without one plea
But that thy blood was shed for me,
And that thou bidd'st me come to thee,
O Lamb of God, I come, I come.

Just as I am, and waiting not
To rid my soul of one dark blot,

To thee, whose blood can cleanse each spot,
O Lamb of God, I come, I come.

Just as I am, though tossed about
With many a conflict, many a doubt,
Fightings and fears within, without,
O Lamb of God, I come, I come.

Just as I am, poor, wretched, blind;
Sight, riches, healing of the mind,
Yea, all I need, in thee to find;
O Lamb of God, I come, I come.

Just as I am! thou wilt receive,
Wilt welcome, pardon, cleanse, relieve;
Because thy promise I believe,
O Lamb of God, I come, I come.

A KNOWLEDGE of the origin of this hymn is an indispensable aid to understanding its meaning. At age thirty-two, the author was stricken with a serious illness that made her a semi-invalid for the rest of her life. Thereafter she struggled with feelings of uselessness and depression, to the point of even doubting that she was a Christian. During an ongoing exchange with a traveling pastor from Switzerland, she expressed the feeling that she needed to clean up her life before coming to Christ. The pastor encouraged her to "come just as you are." Charlotte Elliott was converted that very day. A dozen years later, on a day when she was left behind in the house while others were busy at a church bazaar, she recalled what her sister called "the birthday of her soul to true spiritual life and peace" and penned her most famous hymn.

The theme of the poem is coming to Christ for salvation

from sin. Certain very powerful and universal feelings motivate that journey: craving for acceptance, longing for release from sin's condemnation, hunger for lasting security and provision, and eagerness to end resistance and flee to the only sure satisfaction. The motion of the soul that the poem encapsulates is surrender to divine love in a moment of complete trust.

It is no surprise that this hymn is the most frequently used invitation hymn at evangelistic meetings, because it belongs to the genre of the invitation. Each stanza follows the same paradigm: receiving an invitation, contemplating the nature of the invitation, and accepting the invitation.

In the opening phrase of each stanza, the speaker in the poem rehearses the invitation ("just as I am"), letting it register or "sink in." It is a version of our common invitation to "come as you are." In real life, the appeal of such an invitation is that it is easy—we do not need to bring food or even dress up. In the context of this poem, the "just as you are" principle embodies an important theological meaning—namely, that the sinner brings no merit that can earn salvation. Once the invitation has registered with us, the next two and half lines of each stanza give further details of the invitation that has been extended. The last line, a refrain, is an enthusiastic acceptance of the invitation.

Because of this poem's nearly universal use as a hymn of invitation at evangelistic services, we have been conditioned to assimilate it as an invitation to conversion. But the hymn is also regularly sung at communion services, and this provides an additional avenue to understanding it. The Puritans developed elaborate preparatory exercises for partaking of communion, and the genre of the Puritan preparatory can shine a helpful light on this hymnic poem. Within the context of receiving the invitation to communion and accepting that invitation, the middle part of each stanza is a contemplation of the two essential truths that meet in the sacrament of communion: the sinfulness of the communicant and the redemptive acts of Christ that counteract that sinfulness. If we understand those two things, we can accept the invitation to come to Christ at the Lord's Supper.

C OMING to Christ is the theme of this poem. The most famous invitation to come to Jesus was uttered by Jesus himself:

> Come to me, all who labor and are heavy laden, and I will give you rest. Take my yoke upon you, and learn from me, for I am gentle and lowly in heart, and you will find rest for your souls. (Matt. 11:28–29)

And Can It Be?

Charles Wesley (1707–1788)

And can it be that I should gain
An interest in the Savior's blood?
Died he for me, who caused his pain?
For me, who Him to death pursued?
Amazing love! how can it be
That Thou, my God, shouldst die for me?

'Tis mystery all! The Immortal dies!
Who can explore his strange design?

In vain the firstborn seraph tries
To sound the depths of love divine!
'Tis mercy all! let earth adore,
Let angel minds inquire no more.

He left His Father's throne above,
So free, so infinite his grace;
Emptied Himself of all but love,
And bled for Adam's helpless race:
'Tis mercy all, immense and free;
For, O my God, it found out me.

Long my imprisoned spirit lay
Fast bound in sin and nature's night;
Thine eye diffused a quickening ray,
I woke, the dungeon flamed with light;
My chains fell off, my heart was free,
I rose, went forth, and followed Thee.

No condemnation now I dread;
Jesus, and all in him, is mine!
Alive in him, my living head,
And clothed in righteousness divine,
Bold I approach the eternal throne,
And claim the crown, through Christ my own.

T HIS text is such a heartfelt statement of evangelical faith, and is so familiar to the masses, that it is a surprise to learn upon analyzing it that it is a very poetic text. It not only expresses the white heat of spiritual emotion but also pushes the upper realms of poetic ecstasy. The poem is a song of the soul set free.

The best game plan for explicating this poem is to progress stanza by stanza. The keynote of the opening stanza—a feeling of amazement—is encapsulated in the exclamation "amazing love!" This stanza consists of four questions—a rhetorical form that in this context expresses amazement bordering on incredulity. The poet drives that point home by using the nearly identical formulas "can it be" and "how can it be." The amazement centers not on the objective fact of the atoning death of Christ but rather that it was "for me"—a phrase that appears three times and probably grows out of Wesley's reading of Martin Luther's commentary on Galatians around the time of the poem's composition.

The emotional and exclamatory mode carries forward into the second stanza. Two exclamations carry the emotional argument: "'Tis mystery all!" and "'Tis mercy all!" The stanza is built around a narrative thread in which the poet imagines angels attempting to explore God's love but admitting defeat in the effort. The opening line, moreover, delivers a bold paradox of "the Immortal" (Christ as God) dying (at the crucifixion).

Knowing that a feeling of ecstasy cannot be maintained indefinitely, the poet next leaves the exclamatory rhetoric behind and gives us two stanzas in the narrative mode. Stanza 3 tells the story of Christ's incarnation and passion (his atoning death). The fourth stanza narrates the conversion of the speaker (an Everyman and Everywoman figure). This stanza brilliantly draws from the story of Peter's rescue from prison by an angel (see Acts 12:6–11) and transforms it into a metaphoric account of personal conversion or salvation.

The concluding stanza represents the familiar eschatological turn of many hymns, as the speaker shifts focus to the future and celebrates a heavenly existence made possible through union with Christ. Every line in this poem can be related to familiar Bible verses, but perhaps the most obvious one is the line that reads "no condemnation now I dread," which echoes Romans 8:1: "There is therefore now no condemnation for those who are in Christ Jesus."

As we cast a retrospective look at what we have covered, we can see that this poem is an extended meditation on God's saving love for the sinner. That is the prism that the poem turns in the light. One strand in the poem's tapestry is a series of theological statements about Christ's substitutionary atonement and the divine love that it expresses. In fact, the poem is a brief primer (a statement of first principles) about redemption. Balancing this Christocentric element is a taking stock of the personal story of being saved from sin and death, with emphasis on human unworthiness. The title of a classic by John Murray is a good summary of the twofold thrust of the poem: *Redemption Accomplished and Applied*. Overall, the poem is built around a central contrast between divine generosity and the surprise that sinners feel when they are saved in spite of who they are.

A s we will see with many poems in this anthology, this one contains so many different biblical allusions that it is difficult to choose a single devotional passage as collaborative reading. Nonetheless, the poem's sentiment that salvation is too amazing to be fully understood finds a parallel in Ephesians 3:17–19:

> . . . So that Christ may dwell in your hearts through faith—
> that you . . . [may] comprehend with all the saints what is the
> breadth and length and height and depth, and . . . know the
> love of Christ that surpasses knowledge.

How Firm a Foundation

Author Unknown (1787)

How firm a foundation, ye saints of the Lord,
Is laid for your faith in his excellent Word!
What more can he say than to you he hath said,
To you who for refuge to Jesus have fled?

Fear not, I am with thee, O be not dismayed;
For I am thy God, and will still give thee aid;
I'll strengthen thee, help thee, and cause thee to stand,
Upheld by my righteous, omnipotent hand.

When through the deep waters I call thee to go,
The rivers of sorrow shall not overflow;
For I will be with thee thy troubles to bless,
And sanctify to thee thy deepest distress.

When through fiery trials thy pathway shall lie,
My grace, all sufficient, shall be thy supply;
The flame shall not hurt thee; I only design
Thy dross to consume, and thy gold to refine.

The soul that on Jesus hath leaned for repose,
I will not, I will not desert to his foes;

That soul, though all hell should endeavor to shake,
I'll never, no, never, no, never forsake.

W HEN this hymn was first published by a Baptist minister in London in 1787, it was ascribed to an unidentified "K---." The most noteworthy feature of the poem is the large number of biblical allusions that feed into the text—something that ties in beautifully with the central motif stated right at the outset: namely, the foundation for living that believers can find in the words of Scripture. Once the opening pair of lines has asserted that premise, the entire rest of the poem is an elaboration of it.

In addition to the mosaic of biblical references that make up the poetic texture, there are important rhetorical techniques at work here. For example, after the poem has asserted its thesis in the first two lines, the next two lines address a rhetorical question directly to the reader. A rhetorical question is asked to elicit not information but assent. Readers and singers intuitively answer the question "What more . . . ?" with an understood "Nothing more," and in that very answer they are agreeing with the premise that the poet has asserted.

A second rhetorical technique in the poem is something that is possible to overlook as our attention is focused on the succession of promises from Scripture that passes before us. The poet has arranged his meditation in such a way that everything that appears in the poem after the opening stanza is understood to be a speech addressed by God directly to the reader. As the assurances continue to unfold, we begin to assimilate the words of God as promises to us, with the aggregate eventually seeming like a contract that God is making with us. All we need to do is to sign the contract with our belief.

Identifying the wealth of biblical allusions in this poem might initially seem overwhelming, but an additional strategy makes such analysis more manageable: the general procedure of the poet is to build individual stanzas around one or two biblical passages. Looking up the following biblical passages will enhance our experience of their accompanying stanzas: for the second stanza, Isaiah 41:10; for the third stanza, Isaiah 43:2; for the fourth stanza, 2 Corinthians 12:9 and 1 Peter 4:12–13; for the final stanza, Deuteronomy 31:6.

We should note, finally, the context in which the poem's exuberant promises of encouragement are set. The promises are directed to people in distress. The people addressed by God are those who are dismayed (stanza 2), passing through deep waters (stanza 3), being purified in fire (stanza 4), and being attacked by foes (final stanza). To adapt the title of a Puritan classic, this poem is a lifting up for the downcast.

T HIS poem takes as its subject the promises of God for the believer. The New Testament phrase about God's "precious and very great promises" comes naturally to mind. Here is the passage that contains that phrase and much in addition:

> His divine power has granted to us all things that pertain to life and godliness, through the knowledge of him who called us to his own glory and excellence, by which he has granted to us his precious and very great promises, so that through them you may become partakers of the divine nature. (2 Peter 1:3–4)

Crown Him with Many Crowns

Matthew Bridges (1800–1894);
Godfrey Thring (1823–1903)

Crown him with many crowns,
The Lamb upon his throne;
Hark! how the heavenly anthem drowns
All music but its own:
Awake, my soul, and sing
Of him who died for thee,
And hail him as thy matchless King
Through all eternity.

Crown him the Lord of life,
Who triumphed o'er the grave,
And rose victorious in the strife
For those he came to save;
His glories now we sing
Who died, and rose on high.
Who died, eternal life to bring
And lives that death may die.

Crown him the Lord of love;
Behold his hands and side,
Rich wounds, yet visible above,

In beauty glorified:
No angel in the sky
Can fully bear that sight,
But downward bends his burning eye
At mysteries so bright.

Crown him the Lord of peace,
Whose power a scepter sways
From pole to pole, that wars may cease,
Absorbed in prayer and praise;
His reign shall know no end,
And round his pierced feet,
Fair flowers of Paradise extend
Their fragrance ever sweet.

Crown him the Lord of years,
The Potentate of time,
Creator of the rolling spheres,
Ineffably sublime;
All hail, Redeemer, hail!
For thou hast died for me;
Thy praise shall never, never fail
Throughout eternity.

B EFORE we explore this hymn as a poem, we need to know a
few facts about it. The first version of this hymn was published in 1851 and consisted of six stanzas. The author was Matthew Bridges, who began life as an Anglican and then converted
to Roman Catholicism during a Catholic revival in the Victorian
era known as the Oxford Movement. Some of the stanzas were
so thoroughly rooted in Roman Catholicism as to be obscure
and even unintelligible to Protestants. In 1874, therefore, an
Anglican clergyman and hymn writer named Godfrey Thring

published a hymn with six parallel verses modeled on the same motif of crowning Jesus as "Lord of . . ." Soon thereafter congregations began to "mix and match" the best stanzas from both hymns. In the version printed above, the second stanza is by Thring and the others by Bridges.

Something also needs to be said about misguided criticisms of this poem's "unbiblical imagery," which are based on interpreting its command to crown Jesus literally. This is figurative language, not literal. First, who is being commanded to crown Jesus? Probably the whole company of believers, in which case it is an example of a figure of speech known as apostrophe—a standard way of expressing strong feeling. To crown is here a metaphoric action. It means to exalt, to honor, to revere. Just as an earthly beloved is said to be queen of a man's heart, to crown Jesus means to make him king of our lives.

The most obvious artistic triumph of this poem lies in the area of rhetoric—seen here most prominently in the patterned arrangement of the content. The opening line of every stanza employs a repeated formula that consists of a command to "crown him . . ." The first stanza is generalized ("with many crowns"), and every subsequent stanza presents a more specific reason to crown Jesus, employing the fixed formula "Lord of . . ." Each opening line, moreover, announces the topic that the rest of the stanza will elaborate. This careful patterning is a display of artistry and beauty.

The unifying theme is Christ's worthiness to be crowned in our hearts, souls, and lives. The individual stanzas are variations on that theme, stating reasons why Jesus deserves to be crowned. The theme is announced in the first stanza, and the variations after that praise Jesus as the bringer of eternal life, love, peace, and victory over time and mortality. Within each stanza, the assertions that unfold can be analyzed as variations on the theme that is announced in each opening line.

Slow reading and pondering of the poem will reveal its verbal beauty and the aphoristic quality of its language. That same careful attention will show a continuous thread of exaltation and transcendence, which emphasizes the eternal and heavenly.

T HE point of origin for this poem is the exalted visions of Jesus in heaven found in the book of Revelation. Here is one of those visions:

> And whenever the living creatures give glory and honor and thanks to him who is seated on the throne, who lives forever and ever, the twenty-four elders fall down before him who is seated on the throne and worship him who lives forever and ever. They cast their crowns before the throne, saying,
>
> "Worthy are you, our Lord and God,
>   to receive glory and honor and power." (Rev. 4:9–11)

All Hail the Power of Jesus' Name

Edward Perronet (1726–1792)

All hail the power of Jesus' name!
Let angels prostrate fall;
Bring forth the royal diadem,
And crown him Lord of all.

Crown him, ye martyrs of your God
Who from his altar call;
Extol the stem of Jesse's rod,
And crown him Lord of all.

Ye seed of Israel's chosen race,
Ye ransomed of the fall,
Hail him who saves you by his grace,
And crown him Lord of all.

Sinners, whose love can ne'er forget
The wormwood and the gall,
Go spread your trophies at his feet,
And crown him Lord of all.

Let every kindred, every tribe,
On this terrestrial ball,

To him all majesty ascribe,
And crown him Lord of all.

O that with yonder sacred throng
We at his feet may fall;
We'll join the everlasting song,
And crown him Lord of all.

T HE unifying topic of this poem is the kingship of Jesus. The theme or interpretive slant that the poem takes *toward* this topic is that because Jesus is king, he is worthy of the praise and homage of every believing soul. The central image pattern that supports and carries this theme is the imagery of kingship. Every stanza employs this imagery in multiple ways, clinching the pattern with the concluding refrain line "and crown him Lord of all." The gestures of homage to a king (saying "all hail" when he appears, falling prostrate before him, spreading trophies at his feet, and so on) are foreign to most moderns, but instead of lamenting the archaic nature of the references, we need to give ourselves to doing what we do whenever we read literature from a past era—namely, acquainting ourselves with the customs that once prevailed.

With the central motif so firmly foregrounded, we are in no danger of losing sight of it. What requires closer analysis is the sequence of variations on the central theme. In the order of their appearance, stanza by stanza, the variations on the theme are as follows: angels must crown Jesus as king because of the power of his name; martyrs must extol Jesus as Lord; those who have been chosen to be saved by God's grace must crown Jesus as supreme; sinners who remember Jesus' death must submit their trophies (i.e. worldly accomplishments) to Jesus' rule; every earthly inhabitant must ascribe royal majesty to Jesus; the company of the redeemed will acknowledge Jesus as Lord in their everlasting life in heaven. The poem thus possesses a pleasing variety and comprehensiveness within a unifying framework that could easily become monotonous.

Two separate parts of the Bible feed into the poem and determine its form and content. One is the Old Testament psalm of praise to God. An immediate evidence of this is the way in which the entire poem is a series of commands to praise Jesus as king, just as a standard part of the Old Testament psalm of praise is the command for angels and people to praise God. Second, the psalms of praise state reasons why we should praise God; in this poem, we can infer the reasons for praising God. Finally, numerous psalms (not only the praise psalms) portray God as being king not only of the Israelites but also of the universe—a motif that this poem captures in its repeated phrase "Lord of all."

Additionally, this poem is modeled on multiple throne room scenes in the book of Revelation (see, for example, Rev. 4; 5:6–14; 7:9–17). These heavenly visions are filled with the same imagery that we find in this hymnic poem: images of a throne, of falling down before the throne, of ascribing honor to God seated on the throne, of casting crowns before God, and so on. In the poem, of course, the act of crowning is a figurative act, signifying the paying of allegiance and honor to God and exalting him to a position of primacy. At this personal level, the refrain line, "Crown him Lord of all," acquires a second meaning in addition to the universality of Christ's kingship as noted above: to crown Jesus "Lord of all" means to make him Lord of everything in one's life.

T HIS poem issues a series of commands to exalt Jesus as king. Philippians 2:9–11 uses similar imagery to assert that God the Father has likewise elevated Jesus to a position of ultimate worthiness:

Therefore God has highly exalted him and bestowed on him the name that is above every name, so that at the name of Jesus every knee should bow, in heaven and on earth and under the earth, and every tongue confess that Jesus Christ is Lord, to the glory of God the Father.

O Worship the King

Sir Robert Grant (1779–1838)

O worship the King all glorious above,
O gratefully sing his power and his love;
Our shield and defender, the Ancient of Days,
Pavilioned in splendor, and girded with praise.

O tell of his might, O sing of his grace,
Whose robe is the light, whose canopy space.
His chariots of wrath the deep thunderclouds form,
And dark is his path on the wings of the storm.

The earth with its store of wonders untold,
Almighty, thy power hath founded of old,
Hath stablished it fast by a changeless decree,
And round it hath cast, like a mantle, the sea.

Thy bountiful care what tongue can recite?
It breathes in the air; it shines in the light;
It streams from the hills; it descends to the plain,
And sweetly distils in the dew and the rain.

Frail children of dust, and feeble as frail,
In thee do we trust, nor find thee to fail;
Thy mercies how tender, how firm to the end,
Our maker, defender, redeemer, and friend!

O measureless might! ineffable love!
While angels delight to hymn thee above,
The humbler creation, though feeble their lays,
With true adoration shall lisp to thy praise.

T HIS poem is a song of praise—a genre that comes straight from the Old Testament Psalter. It incorporates several leading features of that genre, including a call to praise, a catalog of praiseworthy divine acts, and the presence of exalted epithets for God. The opening line sets the agenda for the entire poem: it identifies the poem's object as a glorious and transcendent King and establishes the poem's purpose as an act of worship or adoration. These two aspects are reflected in the pronouns that are used for God: in the first two stanzas God is referenced in the third person ("his"), in keeping with his transcendence, and in the rest of the poem God is addressed directly ("thy," "thee"), in a personal and prayer-like stance.

Each stanza has its task to perform in the unfolding progression. The opening stanza is an introduction to God's exalted position as king and to the theme of worship and praise. The general (but not rigid) arrangement then unfolds according to the following topics: God's divine might, the glory of God seen in his creation of the world, God's care or providence toward the created order, and the fatherly provision of God toward frail humanity. Rounding off the poem with a note of closure, the final stanza is like the first in exalting God's divine transcendence (captured by the word *above*) and expressing the response of the believing soul in praise. The poem's organization is like a picture that is framed.

The dominant pattern of imagery comes from nature. Since the poem is an ode, it evokes the sublime aspects of nature as a "language" for portraying the power of God. Nature is portrayed metaphorically—for example, light becomes a robe that God wears, and the sky above a canopy. Analyzing the aptness or logic of the comparisons in the poem can be an avenue toward experiencing the creativity of the poet.

Two additional stylistic features are part of the total effect of the poem. One is the abundance of epithets that both exalt God and characterize him: "shield and defender," "Ancient of Days," "maker," "ineffable love." The poem also contains five examples of a stylistic trait called "the vocative O"—for example, "O worship" and "O measureless might." The effect is that of an exclamation, and the technique appears in formal discourse.

T HE first three stanzas of this poem strike us as somehow familiar. That is because they are modeled on the opening of Psalm 104 (a nature poem):

> Bless the LORD, O my soul!
> O LORD my God, you are very great!
> You are clothed with splendor and majesty,
>> covering yourself with light as with a garment,
>> stretching out the heavens like a tent.
> He lays the beams of his chambers on the waters;
> he makes the clouds his chariot;
>> he rides on the wings of the wind;

he makes his messengers winds,
   his ministers a flaming fire.

He set the earth on its foundations,
   so that it should never be moved.
You covered it with the deep as with a garment. (vv. 1–6)

Come, Thou Fount of Every Blessing

Robert Robinson (1735–1790)

Come, thou fount of every blessing,
Tune my heart to sing thy grace;
Streams of mercy, never ceasing,
Call for songs of loudest praise;
Teach me some melodious sonnet,
Sung by flaming tongues above;
Praise the mount! I'm fixed upon it,
Mount of God's unchanging love.

Here I raise my Ebenezer;
Hither by thy help I'm come;
And I hope, by thy good pleasure,
Safely to arrive at home.
Jesus sought me when a stranger,

Wandering from the fold of God:
He, to rescue me from danger,
Interposed his precious blood.

O to grace how great a debtor
Daily I'm constrained to be;
Let that grace now, like a fetter,
Bind my wandering heart to thee.
Prone to wander, Lord, I feel it,
Prone to leave the God I love;
Here's my heart, O take and seal it,
Seal it for thy courts above.

R EFERENCES in this poem to being a debtor to grace, wandering far from God, and raising a symbolic Ebenezer to mark progress in the spiritual life will fall into place if we know something about the author and the circumstances of the hymn's composition. In his late teen years, the author was a drifter on the streets of London, roving with a gang of hoodlums. At age nineteen he resolved to hear George Whitefield preach, and under the influence of Whitefield's sermon based on Matthew 3:7 (with its warning about fleeing the wrath to come), Robinson was converted and became a dissenting (non-Anglican) minister. Just two years after his conversion, in 1757, he penned this famous hymn.

We can profitably pause to reflect on the opening word of the poem. A summons to "come" is a hymnic convention. What is constant in such far-ranging invitations or petitions is a stance of wishing to receive some desired end that the speaker himself or herself cannot supply. As we ponder the nature of what is desired in the opening stanza of this hymn, we are somewhat surprised. The speaker directs his petition to "the fount of every blessing," which is surely God. But what does the speaker desire from God? As the opening stanza unfolds, it turns out that we have a spiritualized version of the classical invocation to a muse to inspire a poet to compose.

References to "some melodious sonnet," to being fixed on a mountain of God's love, to raising an Ebenezer, and to divine grace being a fetter (a chain or iron weight to keep a prisoner constrained) to prevent wandering alert us that this is a very poetic composition. Instead of resisting this, we should relish it and rise to the challenge. All we need to do is take the time to analyze the images and metaphors and look up words in a dictionary where necessary. These are the ordinary demands that poetry makes on us by requiring a "slow read."

The organized flow of thought and feeling in this poem is as follows: The entire opening stanza is a request for inspiration in order to compose a song, along with hints about the content of the composition. The second stanza changes the subject completely, being a narrative of the speaker's (and our) process of coming to faith in Jesus as Savior. This is nothing less than an archetypal rescue—one made possible by Jesus interposing his precious blood on our behalf. The third stanza has its own distinct subject as well, being a meditation on how much we owe to God's grace, and including petitions for God to take permanent possession of our souls.

Since this poem has become a focal point of a contemporary movement to dilute the poetic quality of the great hymns on the premise that we should allow people to remain at their current low level of knowledge, this is a good occasion for us to resolve not to dumb down the great hymnic treasures from the past. Raising an Ebenezer is an allusion to a famous biblical event recorded in 1 Samuel 7. When God delivered the Israelites from an attack by the Philistines, Samuel set up a stone that he called Ebenezer ("stone of help"), saying, "Hitherto hath the LORD helped us" (v. 12 KJV). To raise an Ebenezer is to take stock, in a spirit of gratitude, of what God has achieved in our lives up to the present moment. As for the statement that Christ "interposed his precious blood," the weighty word *interpose* is a wonderful, theologically laden word that denotes intervention between sinners and their condemnation. As the Greek writer Aristophanes wrote, "High thoughts must have high language."

T HE overall thrust of this poem is to celebrate what God has done for sinners and the gratitude that they feel for their deliverance. Ephesians 2:4–7 sounds the same notes:

> But God, being rich in mercy, because of the great love with which he loved us, even when we were dead in our trespasses, made us alive together with Christ—by grace you have been saved—and raised us up with him and seated us with him in the heavenly places in Christ Jesus, so that in the coming ages he might show the immeasurable riches of his grace in kindness toward us in Christ Jesus.

Love Divine, All Loves Excelling

Charles Wesley (1707–1788)

Love Divine, all loves excelling,
Joy of heaven, to earth come down,
Fix in us thy humble dwelling,
All thy faithful mercies crown:
Jesus, thou art all compassion,
Pure, unbounded love thou art;
Visit us with thy salvation,
Enter every trembling heart.

Breathe, O breathe thy loving Spirit
Into every troubled breast;
Let us all in thee inherit,
Let us find the promised rest;
Take away the love of sinning;
Alpha and Omega be;
End of faith, as its beginning,
Set our hearts at liberty.

Come, Almighty to deliver,
Let us all thy life receive;
Suddenly return, and never,
Never more thy temples leave.
Thee we would be always blessing,

Serve thee as thy hosts above,
Pray, and praise thee, without ceasing,
Glory in thy perfect love.

Finish, then, thy new creation;
Pure and spotless let us be;
Let us see thy great salvation
Perfectly restored in thee;
Changed from glory into glory,
Till in heaven we take our place,
Till we cast our crowns before thee,
Lost in wonder, love and praise.

C HARLES Wesley's best-known hymns are signature Methodist hymns, and this one is an example. Its religious temperament and implied doctrine belong to Methodism. Nonetheless,
"Love Divine" is included in so many hymnals (rivaling even
"Amazing Grace") that we can safely conclude that it transcends
denominational distinctives. The poem is cast into the form of a
prayer, and the object of address keeps changing. Many hymnic
poems follow a Trinitarian pattern, and the stanzas in this poem
are addressed, respectively, to Jesus, the Holy Spirit, the Father,
and the complete Godhead (an inference).

Many hymns have such striking openings that they sometimes lull us into incorrectly assuming that the entire poem is
an extension of the opening line or two. The first two lines of
this hymnic poem are a series of epithets or titles that form an
opening invocation. They exalt Jesus in such enrapturing language that they might lead us to assume that this extended
prayer is a praise poem. But it is not. Except for the opening
lines, this poem is an extended prayer of petition, as the speaker
makes a series of requests or supplications to God. The verbs are

not declarative but imperative. The speaker is not a worshiper engaged in praise of God but rather the archetypal suppliant making requests to God. Once we have this in focus, several avenues to meditation and analysis open up.

One is to note (and perhaps compile a list of) the things for which the speaker (and we with him) asks. The list is a many-sided one, as every line or pair of lines states a separate need or desire. Then we can proceed to look for clusters of related subjects. Examples are salvation of soul, sanctification, and God's presence in one's moment-by-moment experience.

In addition to presenting an inventory of supplications, the poem paints an implied portrait of two people. One is the speaker as the archetypal Everyman and Everywoman. A list of requests such as we find in this poem represents a picture of what the suppliant feels most in need of, and these needs, in turn, are a means of characterization. For example, the poem speaks of a trembling heart and a troubled breast—what do we infer these are? We read about the love of sinning and hearts that need to be set at liberty; from this we infer things about the human condition that require an infusion of grace.

The poem also paints a portrait of God. The temperament of the speaker is emotionally charged, and we accordingly find effusive claims made for the love of God and for the overpowering nature of his visitations to the human heart and his supreme worthiness to be worshiped here and in heaven.

As a footnote to this energetic tone, we might note the poem's search for superlatives. On a spiritual plane, the speaker wants it all. He creates a vocabulary of ecstasy with such words as *all*, *every*, *always*, *without ceasing*, *perfect*, and *perfectly*. The speaker expresses a wish not simply to worship God eternally but to be "lost in wonder, love and praise." The poem has a flavor all its own.

W HEN we read this poem at a meditative pace, nearly every line reminds us of one or more biblical verses. This variety makes any choice of collaborative reading a little arbitrary, but the following excerpts from Psalm 51 parallel the petitions made in Wesley's poem:

> Have mercy on me, O God,
>> according to your steadfast love;
>
> . . . .
>
> Create in me a clean heart, O God,
>> and renew a right spirit within me.
> Cast me not away from your presence,
>> and take not your Holy Spirit from me.
> Restore to me the joy of your salvation,
>> and uphold me with a willing spirit. (vv. 1, 10–12)

Like a River Glorious

Frances Ridley Havergal (1836–1879)

Like a river glorious
Is God's perfect peace,
Over all victorious
In its bright increase;

Perfect, yet it floweth
Fuller every day
Perfect, yet it groweth
Deeper all the way.

Hidden in the hollow
Of his blessed hand,
Never foe can follow,
Never traitor stand;
Not a surge of worry,
Not a shade of care,
Not a blast of hurry
Touch the spirit there.

Every joy or trial
Falleth from above,
Traced upon our dial
By the Sun of Love.
We may trust him fully
All for us to do;
They who trust him wholly
Find him wholly true.

Refrain
Stayed upon Jehovah,
Hearts are fully blest,
Finding, as he promised,
Perfect peace and rest.

T HE right way to appropriate the literary richness of this hymnic poem is to apply an archetypal approach to it. Archetypes are the universal master images that recur throughout literature. They are nothing less than the building blocks of the literary imagination. But the reason they recur in literature is that they make up the groundwork of life in the real world.

The first archetype that we encounter in this poem is the peaceful river. The starting point for analyzing an archetype is to meditate on our own experiences of that archetype—in this case the smoothly flowing, peaceful, life-giving river. What feelings are evoked in us when we walk beside a calm river or cross it on a bridge? After we consider this, we can analyze what qualities of a river evoke those feelings. The details with which Frances Havergal surrounds the river in her opening stanza serve as a guide on this path of analysis.

Once we have taken stock of our own life experiences of the archetypal peaceful river, our next step is to place this instance of the archetype into our literary experience as a whole. We should start with the Bible, because it is the main repository of the literary archetypes of the Western imagination. Our memory reaches out to the river whose streams make glad the city of God in Psalm 46:4, to the still waters of Psalm 23:2, and to the river that flows from the throne of God lined with the tree of life on its sides (see Rev. 22:1–2). Verses like these are only the tip of the iceberg—and there is no good reason to stop with the Bible, since other literary examples also feed into our experience of a text.

The poem's second stanza is built around the archetypal safe place or haven. This stanza places one example before us (the hollow of a hand), but we can multiply our own examples of places where we feel totally protected from threats to our safety and well-being. In this stanza, too, the author does a magnificent job of acting as a travel guide to help us unpack the dimensions of the archetypal safe place and the threats that make such sanctuary necessary. The third stanza has its own image or metaphor as well—namely, a sundial on which the sun falls and enables people to trace the time of day. Havergal manages the image in such a way as to stress the concept of a predictable pattern that is traced by a source in the sky (a metaphor for divine providence).

The refrain is a summary of all three stanzas, and there are latent archetypes here as well: fixing securely on a trusted person, being blest, fulfillment of promise, and a search that leads to finding the object of the quest.

This poem is so "over the top" in its assertions of trust and calm that we naturally wonder if the statements might be overly facile or glib. That is where the biographical context of this poem packs a punch. The author suffered from frail health virtually her entire life of forty-two years. In the two years before this poem was written in 1876, the author (a) nearly died from a lingering illness she contracted while traveling in Wales, (b) had her financial prospects struck down when an American publisher who had planned to circulate her writings in the United States, and who owned the sole rights to them, went bankrupt, and (c) had the only copy of a book that was ready for publication perish in a fire.

T HIS poem extends outward to many verses in the Bible. In addition to Isaiah 26:3 ("You keep him in perfect peace whose mind is stayed on you"), Isaiah 66:12 is particularly relevant:

> For thus says the LORD:
> "Behold, I will extend peace to her like a river,
> and the glory of the nations like an overflowing stream."

In Christ Alone

Keith Getty (b. 1974) and Stuart Townend (b. 1963)

In Christ alone my hope is found;
He is my light, my strength, my song,
This cornerstone, this solid ground,
Firm through the fiercest drought and storm.
What heights of love, what depths of peace,
When fears are stilled, when strivings cease!
My comforter, my all in all—
Here in the love of Christ I stand.

In Christ alone, who took on flesh,
Fullness of God in helpless babe!
This gift of love and righteousness,
Scorned by the ones He came to save.
Till on that cross as Jesus died,
The wrath of God was satisfied;
For every sin on Him was laid—
Here in the death of Christ I live.

There in the ground His body lay,
Light of the world by darkness slain;
Then bursting forth in glorious day,
Up from the grave He rose again!

And as He stands in victory,
Sin's curse has lost its grip on me;
For I am His and He is mine—
Bought with the precious blood of Christ.

No guilt in life, no fear in death—
This is the power of Christ in me;
From life's first cry to final breath,
Jesus commands my destiny.
No power of hell, no scheme of man,
Can ever pluck me from His hand;
Till He returns or calls me home—
Here in the power of Christ I'll stand.

THIS poem is noteworthy for its exalted tone and its weighty content. It celebrates something big, and accordingly it quickly catches us up in the magnitude of what is presented. The twin themes of the poem are (a) what Christ has accomplished and (b) the certainties that these accomplishments have brought into the speaker's life. The poem thus looks both outward to the redemptive life of Christ and inward to the speaker's mind, feelings, and life. Of course, as readers we allow the speaker's feelings to be ours as well.

The Christocentric focus of the poem is signaled by the opening phrase, which is repeated at the start of the second stanza: "In Christ alone." The closing line of each stanza reiterates how the speaker stands and lives in the love, death, blood, and power of Christ (the topics of the respective closing lines).

The stanzaic arrangement of any poem results in a packaging of the material in distinct units, and this poem runs true to form. The opening stanza celebrates in broad strokes and generalized images what Christ has accomplished and what this has meant in the life of the speaker. The imagery of the middle two stanzas is more specific, consisting primarily of allusions to the redemptive life, death, and resurrection of Jesus. The final stanza shifts the focus from what Christ has done to its implications in the believer's life. It is a stanza of application, a song of confidence, and an inventory of what the speaker possesses in Christ.

The modern spirit of the poem is seen in its fluid arrangement. Although there is a loose division of duties between what Christ has accomplished (in stanzas 1–3) and an introspective "taking stock" of how this applies to the speaker (in stanza 4), a careful look shows that the introspective note finds its way into every stanza.

Writing teachers instill in their students the maxim that the writer's task is "to show rather than tell"—that is, to incarnate a subject in concrete images. The poetic texture of this poem consists of imagery and figures of speech (including allusion), and the task that this lays on the reader is to unpack the meanings of the images.

Anyone familiar with ancient literature (including the Psalms) can see at a glance that the genre of this poem is the song of victory (which is also called the song of thanksgiving). Such poems are in effect battlefield celebrations of victory. Psalm 18 is an example. There is a tone of confidence in this genre, which shades off into a genre (which is fully evident in the Bible) known as the boast. This poem is a boast in the manner of Paul's statement that he will "boast . . . in the cross of our Lord Jesus Christ" (Gal. 6:14).

T HIS poem rehearses the treasures that a believer possesses in Christ: the redemptive acts of Christ and the resulting benefits in the believer's life. The so-called thanksgiving section that appears early in the New Testament epistles is likewise an inventory of the treasures that a believer possesses in Christ:

Blessed be the God and Father of our Lord Jesus Christ, who has blessed us in Christ with every spiritual blessing. . . . In him we have redemption through his blood, the forgiveness of our trespasses, according to the riches of his grace, which he lavished upon us. (Eph. 1:3, 7–8)

Rock of Ages

Augustus Toplady (1740–1778)

Rock of Ages, cleft for me
Let me hide myself in thee;
Let the water and the blood,
From thy riven side which flowed,
Be of sin the double cure,
Cleanse me from its guilt and power.

Not the labors of my hands
Can fulfil thy law's demands;
Could my zeal no respite know,
Could my tears for ever flow,
All for sin could not atone;
Thou must save, and thou alone.

Nothing in my hand I bring,
Simply to thy cross I cling;
Naked, come to thee for dress,
Helpless, look to thee for grace;
Foul, I to the fountain fly;
Wash me, Savior, or I die.

While I draw this fleeting breath,
When mine eyelids close in death,
When I soar to worlds unknown,
See thee on thy judgment throne,
Rock of Ages, cleft for me,
Let me hide myself in thee.

A NUMBER of the hymns in this anthology are inseparable from the circumstances of their original composition. "Rock of Ages" is one of these. The story with which the poem is associated is unsubstantiated, but it is part of the "mythology" surrounding the poem. According to the legend, the author, a young cleric at the time, was walking along a road near his village when a thunderstorm struck. He dashed into a depression or cave in the cliffs of a rocky hill. A poem began to form in his mind; and, lacking paper on which to write, he saw a playing card and began to write on that.

The literary foundation on which Toplady has built is the archetypal rock. We are to picture a hill-sized rock with a vertical split or fissure forming a hollow at the bottom. The rock is a prominent biblical archetype and metaphor for God, picturing his stability, permanence, and majesty. Additionally, a rocky cliff can provide protection from either heat or storm. Multiple biblical references to God as a rock and to deliverance provided by a rock can be traced, but for the purposes of this poem an especially important reference is the event narrated in Exodus

33:22, in which God places Moses in "a cleft of the rock" as his glory passes.

The poem gets maximum mileage out of the imagery of being "cleft." *Cleft* is a now-archaic past tense of *cleave*. The verb *cleave*, in turn, can mean both "split open" and "cling to." Both motions merge in the poem, as the speaker implicitly clings to the sides of a hollow that has been split open in a rocky cliff on the side of a hill. Although the word *cleft* appears only in the first and last stanzas, when we read about *clinging* in the third stanza, we can see a process of association going on in the poem's imagery.

As we keep scrutinizing the image patterns, we begin to see the importance of various liquids that are named; and these references, in turn, allude to passages in the Bible. Thus we find the water and blood that flowed from Jesus' side as he hung on the cross, tears of repentance from the speaker, and the divine fountain of cleansing. We also need to be receptive to the consistent technique by which this poem pictures spiritual experience in the form of concrete images: *rock, hide, water, blood, labors of one's hands, tears flowing, empty hands, naked ness requiring dress, fountain, eyelids closing in death, judgment throne.* Poets think in images, and the author of this poem makes the grade.

If we turn from this complex poetic texture to the structure of the poem, we find the following: The opening and closing pairs of lines are identical, giving the poem an envelope or "bookends" structure. After the two-line lead-in, the remainder of the opening stanza is a prayer for cleansing from sin based on the atoning death of Jesus on the cross. The second stanza explains why Christ's atonement is necessary—namely, human inability to earn salvation. The third stanza covers similar territory, shifting the focus, however, from actions that are insufficient to a picture of the sinner as being naked, helpless, and foul.

The final stanza takes an eschatological turn by shifting our gaze to death, heaven, and the final judgment.

Like most hymnic poems, this one is simple enough to be accessible to any believing soul, yet possessed of hidden poetic richness that emerges as we exercise our analytic abilities as close readers of a poetic text.

T HE opening and closing image of an evocative "rock of ages" exerts a controlling presence throughout the poem, even though it is explicitly evoked only at the beginning and end. Psalm 18:2 is also testimony to the power of the image of God as a rock:

> The LORD is my rock and my fortress and my deliverer,
>   my God, my rock, in whom I take refuge,
>   my shield, and the horn of my salvation, my stronghold.

How Great Thou Art

Stuart K. Hine (1899–1989)

O Lord my God, when I in awesome wonder,
Consider all the worlds Thy hands have made;
I see the stars, I hear the rolling thunder,
Thy power throughout the universe displayed,

Then sings my soul, My Savior God, to Thee,
How great Thou art, How great Thou art.

When through the woods, and forest glades I wander,
And hear the birds sing sweetly in the trees;
When I look down, from lofty mountain grandeur
And see the brook, and feel the gentle breeze,
    Then sings my soul, My Savior God, to Thee,
    How great Thou art, How great Thou art.

And when I think, that God, His Son not sparing,
Sent Him to die, I scarce can take it in—
That on the cross, my burden gladly bearing,
He bled and died to take away my sin,
    Then sings my soul, My Savior God, to Thee,
    How great Thou art, How great Thou art.

When Christ shall come, with shout of acclamation,
And take me home, what joy shall fill my heart,
Then I shall bow, in humble adoration,
And there proclaim: "My God, how great Thou art!"

T HE popularity of this iconic hymn is truly remarkable. A 2013 poll conducted by the British Broadcasting Company showed it to be the all-time favorite hymn in the United Kingdom. In the United States, the origin of the hymn's popularity dates from the middle of the 1950s, when it became the signature song of the Billy Graham crusades. The hymn would never have attained this stature without its poetic qualities.

One of the most obvious poetic strengths of "How Great Thou Art" is its firm organizational pattern. The poem is built on a repetitive design in which each stanza displays the same rhetorical pattern. That pattern consists of a subordinate "when" statement followed by a clause that completes it. In each case, this culminating sentence element begins with the adverb *then*. The technical name for a sentence in which we need to keep reading until we reach the main clause is "suspended sentence structure," and its effect is that we experience increasing expectation and then end with a sense of climax. In this poem, the "when" clauses name what the speaker either observes in nature or contemplates in his mind, and the "then" clauses state a response of either wonder or praise. More specifically, in stanza 1 the speaker *considers* and *sees*; in stanza 2 he *hears*, *looks*, and *feels*; in stanza 3 he *thinks* (that is, meditates on); and in stanza 4 he *imagines* the return of Christ in glory. The poem as a whole thus juxtaposes a strong element of sameness in each stanza with a firm progression and change from stanza to stanza.

The first two stanzas are nature poetry, modeled on the nature poems of the Psalter, which transmute the beauties of nature into praise of God. Behind the stanzas lies Psalm 8, a nature poem in which the poet begins his meditation on nature with the contemplative stance, "When I look at your heavens, the work of your fingers . . ." (v. 3). Nature-writing through the centuries has divided its praises between the sublime and the picturesque, and these two stanzas combine them. We are led to contemplate both the "awesome wonder" of the thunder and stars and the "softer" pleasures of the forest, the bird songs, the brook, and the gentle breeze.

Christian theology has always claimed that God reveals himself in complementary "books": nature, revelation (the Bible), and Christ. After reveling in the book of nature in stanzas 1 and 2, we turn in the third stanza to Christ's great work of redemption, in which the emphasis (as in stanzas 1 and 2) is the wonder of it all ("I scarce can take it in"). And then, in a poem that traverses the whole span of biblical history from Genesis to Revelation, after praising God's power in creation and redemption in Christ, we end in the last stanza with the eschaton (the age to come).

I N the commentary surrounding this poem, Psalm 145 is regularly suggested as a parallel text (if not an actual source). Here are selected verses from that psalm:

> Great is the Lord, and greatly to be praised,
>   and his greatness is unsearchable.
>
> . . . .
>
> The Lord is gracious and merciful,
>   slow to anger and abounding in steadfast love.
> The Lord is good to all,
>   and his mercy is over all that he has made.
>
> All your works shall give thanks to you, O Lord,
>   and all your saints shall bless you! (vv. 3, 8–10)

It Is Well with My Soul

Horatio Spafford (1828–1888)

When peace, like a river, attendeth my way,
When sorrows like sea billows roll;
Whatever my lot, thou hast taught me to say,
It is well, it is well with my soul.

Though Satan should buffet, though trials should come,
Let this blest assurance control,
That Christ has regarded my helpless estate,
And has shed his own blood for my soul.

My sin—O the bliss of this glorious thought!—
My sin, not in part, but the whole,
Is nailed to the cross and I bear it no more;
Praise the Lord, praise the Lord, O my soul!

O Lord, haste the day when the faith shall be sight,
The clouds be rolled back as a scroll,
The trump shall resound and the Lord shall descend;
"Even so"—it is well with my soul.

Refrain
It is well, with my soul.
It is well, it is well, with my soul.

A NUMBER of the poems in this anthology sprang from experiences of great tragedy, and this is one of them. The author and his family were prosperous and revered members of Chicago society in the 1860s and were part of the Presbyterian subculture in that city. Various calamities then struck them, including the loss of a real estate fortune in the Great Chicago Fire of 1871. In 1873, while Horatio remained behind to settle business matters, his wife and four daughters embarked on a ship for Europe. The ship collided with another one, the four daughters drowned as the ship sank in twelve minutes, and, when Mrs. Spafford landed in England, she sent a heart-rending telegram to her husband that began with the words, "Saved alone. What shall I do?" When Horatio sailed to meet her a few days later, he penned his famous hymnic poem on a piece of stationery from a Chicago hotel as he neared the site of the shipwreck.

Surely it is common for people to reflect, while singing this hymn, on who it is to whom they are singing. Are they offering a personal testimony to the congregation? Are they addressing themselves in a form of spiritual "self talk" in the mode of Psalm 103, with its opening statement, "Bless the LORD, O my soul"? The answer is "both"—and, as in all the entries in this anthology, it is useful to remind ourselves of the view that English poet William Wordsworth expressed regarding lyric poems. If a poem expresses truth and beauty, it serves "to rectify [people's] feelings." Whenever the poems in this anthology seem to offer a higher standard than we ourselves feel to be realistically attainable, they nonetheless give us an ideal for which to aim. The feelings expressed in such a poem can help us to correct our own feelings.

As is true of any well-crafted poem, each stanza here has its own poetic task to perform as part of a harmonious whole. Using the contrasting water imagery of a peaceful river and an out-of-control storm at sea, the opening stanza expresses the ideal of contentment, along the lines of Paul's statement about being content in the up-and-down situations of life (see Phil. 4:11–12). From the theme of contentment in stanza 1, we move to the theme of assurance in stanza 2. Stanza 3 then expands upon the last line of stanza 2 ("and has shed his own blood for my soul") by focusing on Christ's dying for our sins, using the metaphor from Colossians 2:14 of nailing the record of sin to the cross. In the concluding stanza, the poem takes the familiar eschatological turn that is almost expected in a hymn, as the focus shifts to the Second Coming, employing familiar apocalyptic imagery of the clouds being rolled back and a trumpet announcing the advent of Christ's return.

The literature of the modern era is the voice of despair. Optimistic expressions are stigmatized as being escapist. But the poetry of Christian affirmation, such as this hymn, is not escapist. What it offers is *an escape from* the defeatism that much of life would impose on us apart from our faith in God.

A s are most poems in this anthology, this one is a network of biblical allusions. This song of spiritual well-being even in the face of the vicissitudes of life is especially reminiscent of the following testimony by the apostle Paul:

> I have learned in whatever situation I am to be content. I know how to be brought low, and I know how to abound. In any and every circumstance, I have learned the secret of facing plenty and hunger, abundance and need. I can do all things through him who strengthens me. (Phil. 4:11–13)

Abide with Me

Henry Lyte (1793–1847)

Abide with me; fast falls the eventide;
The darkness deepens; Lord, with me abide.
When other helpers fail and comforts flee,
Help of the helpless, O abide with me.

Swift to its close ebbs out life's little day;
Earth's joys grow dim, its glories pass away;
Change and decay in all around I see;
O thou who changest not, abide with me.

I need thy presence every passing hour;
What but thy grace can foil the tempter's power?
Who like thyself my guide and stay can be?
Through cloud and sunshine, O abide with me.

I fear no foe, with thee at hand to bless;
Ills have no weight and tears no bitterness.
Where is death's sting? where, grave, thy victory?
I triumph still, if thou abide with me.

Hold thou thy cross before my closing eyes;
Shine through the gloom, and point me to the skies.

Heaven's morning breaks, and earth's vain shadows flee;
In life, in death, O Lord, abide with me.

As a prelude to exploring this hymn, it is important to have before us the history of its reception. While this hymn is *somewhat* known in the United States, in the British Isles it has been one of the most important evangelical hymns for the past two centuries, right up to the present day. Beyond that, it is nothing less than a cultural icon in England. It is sung before two key championship games, the Rugby League Challenge Cup and the FA Cup Finals, which are both played annually at Wembley Stadium in London. It has appeared in movies and television series and has been sung at state funerals and remembrance services and royal weddings. It was also reportedly played by the band as the *Titanic* sank.

The story of the hymn's origin is nearly as dramatic as its history. The author was an Anglican minister who suffered from ill health for most of his life. Three years before his death at the age of fifty-four, he was diagnosed with tuberculosis. Upon preaching his farewell sermon to his congregation, he retired to his room and wrote "Abide with Me." He died a couple of months later, and the hymn was sung at his memorial service.

"Abide with Me" takes impending death as its subject. The poem is a meditation on what it will be like to face our death. The speaker in the poem (and we with him) takes stock of what a person needs when facing death. What we need, according to the poem, is God's presence with us. Thus the hymn belongs to a long meditative tradition in English poetry that is known by the Latin phrase *meditatio mortis* ("meditation on death").

But Lyte's poem is more than a meditation on approaching death. It is constructed as a prayer addressed directly to God and as such is a means by which we can unite our souls to God. More specifically, the phrase that ends every stanza ("abide with me") shows that the essential motion of the poem is a plea for divine companionship. The fear of being abandoned lies within every human soul, and this poem speaks to that fear. In four of the stanzas, the craving for God's companionship occurs in a context of impending death, but the middle stanza broadens the scope and expresses a desire for God's presence in all circumstances—"every passing hour" and "through cloud and sunshine." This is the avenue by which we might ponder why this hymn has proven so universally applicable, being sung not only at funerals but also at sports events and weddings.

There can be no doubt that this poem is a very powerful example of mood poetry. Numerous lines evoke a mood of sadness, which is achieved especially by certain great archetypes, such as sunset, deepening darkness, and closing eyes. These take their place within an overarching awareness that death is near. Certainly much of the poem brings us to the verge of tears, but there is an undercurrent of comfort and hope to serve as a check on our sadness and weeping. The ultimate strength of this poem is its ability to move us deeply.

T HE point of departure for Lyte's poem is the story of Jesus and the two disciples from Emmaus. Lyte turned the following passage (Luke 24:29) to metaphoric use in his poem (in which the end of a day becomes the end of life), and we can extend that by meditating on applications to our own lives:

> They urged him [Jesus] strongly, saying, "Stay with us, for it is toward evening and the day is now far spent." So he went in to stay with them.

Ye Holy Angels Bright

Richard Baxter (1615–1691)

Ye holy angels bright,
Who wait at God's right hand,
Or through the realms of light
Fly at your Lord's command,
Assist our song, or else the theme
Too high doth seem for mortal tongue.

Ye blessed souls at rest,
Who ran this earthly race
And now, from sin released,
Behold your Savior's face,
God's praises sound, as in His light
With sweet delight ye do abound.

Ye saints, who toil below,
Adore your heavenly King,
And onward as ye go
Some joyful anthem sing;
Take what He gives, and praise Him still,
Through good or ill, whoever lives.

My soul, bear thou thy part,
Triumph in God above,

And with a well-tuned heart
Sing thou the songs of love;
Let all thy days till life shall end,
Whate'er He send, be filled with praise.

T HE author of this soaring poem was one of the most important Puritan leaders of the seventeenth century. Richard Baxter was a famous minister and public figure of his day, and he wrote so many books (approximately one hundred seventy books and treatises) that it comes as a surprise that he also found time to write poems and hymns. But he did, and a literary scholar has written a whole book on Baxter as a "Puritan man of letters."

"Ye Holy Angels Bright" is an impeccably organized poem that sweeps us along with its long, flowing sentences. Its genre is known as the doxology: a poem or hymn that commands an audience to praise God. The prototype of the form is Psalm 148. Baxter further follows that psalm's strategy of composing an entire poem around the poetic form known as apostrophe—an address to an absent audience as though it were present and could respond. In further imitation of Psalm 148, Baxter keeps varying the group that is being addressed as the poem unfolds.

The speaker addresses four successive "listeners:" the angels in heaven, believers who have died and now reside in heaven, believers on earth, and the speaker's own soul. Each of these entities receives a stanza of elaboration, which produces a format that wins us with its tidiness. The constant element or theme is the command to praise God. The variations on this theme consist of the changing recipients of the command. Upon analysis, we begin to see the skill with which Baxter adapts the command to praise God to each specific group being addressed.

The first stanza is based on the angelology (the study of

angels) of the day and corresponds to what Baxter's fellow Puritan John Milton did at the conclusion of his sonnet on his blindness. Milton refers to active angels who ceaselessly conduct God's business on earth (who "post [i.e., travel] o'er land and ocean without rest") and to contemplative angels who always attend God's presence in heaven (who "only stand and wait" in God's heavenly court). Baxter likewise begins by naming two categories of angels: those who "wait at God's right hand" and those who "fly" at God's command. These angels are invoked not to praise God themselves but rather to assist the speaker and his fellow humans, in a manner parallel to the classical poets who invoked the muses to inspire their poems.

The second stanza describes the praise of "blessed souls at rest"—that is, glorified believers in heaven. The mention of "souls at rest" is a good reminder that Baxter's most famous devotional book is entitled *The Saints' Everlasting Rest*. The imagery of the stanza corresponds to the heavenly abode of this group: resting, being released from sin, beholding God's face, residing in light, abounding in sweet delight.

The third stanza commands saints below to adore God. The imagery accordingly shifts from heavenly rest to earthly endeavor and includes references to toil, to being below rather than being up in heaven, to traveling onward, and to receiving ill as well as good.

The final stanza turns to self-address, as the speaker (and we with him) speaks to his own soul and commands it to praise God. Careful analysis of the images of the last stanza reveals how skillfully Baxter echoes the images of the previous stanzas, making reference to the transcendent realm ("God above"), to music ("well-tuned heart," "songs of love"), to earthly life ("all thy days"), to life ending in death ("till life shall end"), and to the vicissitudes of earthly life that are governed by providence ("whate'er He send"). Despite the variety among the four groups it addresses, there is a unifying thread of the communion of the saints woven throughout the tapestry.

T HIS poem is what literary scholars label "intertextual," inasmuch as we cannot read it without also thinking of Psalm 148. Here is an excerpt from that poem:

> Praise the LORD!
> Praise the LORD from the heavens;
>> praise him in the heights!
> Praise him, all his angels;
>> praise him, all his hosts!
> . . . .
>
> He [God] has raised up a horn for his people,
>> praise for all his saints,
>> for the people of Israel who are near to him.
> Praise the LORD! (vv. 1–2, 14)

A Mighty Fortress Is Our God

Martin Luther (1483–1546)

A mighty fortress is our God,
A bulwark never failing;
Our helper he amid the flood
Of mortal ills prevailing.
For still our ancient foe
Doth seek to work us woe;
His craft and power are great,
And armed with cruel hate;
On earth is not his equal.

Did we in our own strength confide,
Our striving would be losing,
Were not the right Man on our side,
The Man of God's own choosing.
Dost ask who that may be?
Christ Jesus, it is he;
Lord Sabaoth his name,
From age to age the same,
And he must win the battle.

And though this world, with devils filled,
Should threaten to undo us,

We will not fear, for God hath willed
His truth to triumph through us.
The prince of darkness grim,
We tremble not for him;
His rage we can endure,
For lo! his doom is sure;
One little word shall fell him.

That Word above all earthly powers,
No thanks to them, abideth;
The Spirit and the gifts are ours
Through him who with us sideth;
Let goods and kindred go,
This mortal life also;
The body they may kill:
God's truth abideth still;
His kingdom is forever.

A LTHOUGH there is no consensus regarding the specific occasion in Luther's life that produced this hymn (in fact, there are half a dozen theories about it), the general context is the Protestant Reformation. The hymn is accurately known as "the battle hymn of the Reformation." If we assimilate the words in light of what we know about Luther's life as the foremost Lutheran Reformer, everything falls into place—including a sense of heightened spiritual conflict, the presence of a life-or-death battle, the reality of living in danger even to the point of possible martyrdom, and a sense of confidence that springs from the conviction of belonging to God's cause. A certain all-or-nothing vigor energizes the poem from start to finish.

The first two and half lines allude to the opening verse of Psalm 46. Luther's words are "A mighty fortress is our God, a bulwark never failing; our helper . . ." Psalm 46 begins with the same images: "God is our refuge and strength, a very present help in trouble." This correspondence has led to misleading claims that Luther's entire poem is based on Psalm 46 and even that it is a metrical paraphrase of the psalm. The most that can be claimed is that certain general *qualities* and *motifs* correspond—including a context of extreme conflict that might induce fear, a strong confidence in God's presence in the midst of the conflict that is raging, military imagery, and triumphalist language and tone. At these general levels of correspondence, it is entirely possible that Psalm 46 is the model that influenced Luther as he composed.

At this point, C. S. Lewis's distinction between the Bible as a literary source and a literary influence proves helpful. Lewis famously said that a source gives writers something about which to write, while an influence prompts them to write in a certain way. The source of "A Mighty Fortress" was Luther's stressful and often precarious life as a church Reformer. The imagery and sentiments of Psalm 46 provided Luther with a model (or "influence," in Lewis's formula) for how to express his life's experiences.

Three ingredients form the content of the poem, and they converge in each stanza. They are as follows: (1) the certainty of God's presence and power in the world; (2) the terrible opposition that Christians face in the world; (3) the confidence with which Christians can confront opposition through the strength of God. The battle motif unifies the poem, and God is pronounced the victor. The poem asserts that Christians should have confidence that God will win their battle. Some modern churchgoers profess to feel uncomfortable singing the final verse, but the strength of this poem is that it presents life in extremity and gives us a divine strategy for living boldly in that extremity. At times when the Reformation seemed lost, Luther and his friend Philip Melanchthon would sing Psalm 46.

As many as one hundred English versions of this hymn exist. The familiar one printed above was produced by American Frederick H. Hedge in 1852.

P SALM 46 provided Luther with his inspiration for writing "A Mighty Fortress," and the entire psalm makes excellent collaborative reading for the poem. The following excerpt epitomizes the psalm:

God is our refuge and strength,
    a very present help in trouble.
Therefore we will not fear though the earth gives way,
    though the mountains be moved into the heart of the sea,
though its waters roar and foam,
    though the mountains tremble at its swelling.
. . . .

The LORD of hosts is with us;
    The God of Jacob is our fortress. (vv. 1–3, 7)

Come, Thou Almighty King

Author Unknown (mid-eighteenth century)

Come, thou Almighty King,
Help us thy name to sing,
Help us to praise;
Father, all glorious,
O'er all victorious,
Come, and reign over us,
Ancient of days.

Come, thou Incarnate Word,
Gird on thy mighty sword,
Our prayer attend:
Come and thy people bless,
And give thy word success;
Spirit of holiness,
On us descend.

Come, Holy Comforter,
Thy sacred witness bear
In this glad hour;
Thou who almighty art,
Now rule in every heart,
And ne'er from us depart,
Spirit of power.

To the great One in Three
Eternal praises be,
Hence evermore.
His sovereign majesty
May we in glory see,
And to eternity
Love and adore.

T HE most obvious feature of this poem is its Trinitarian emphasis. The danger, however, in designating a poem with a doctrinal or liturgical label is that it inclines us to see only that aspect of the text. The antidote is to see more than the central aspect while still acknowledging it. Stanza 1 of this poem addresses the "Father," stanza 2 "the Incarnate Word" (the Son), stanza 3 the "Holy Comforter," and stanza 4 "the great One in Three."

In addition to being a Trinitarian poem, this is a worship hymn and poem. The opening lines invoke God's aid to help us sing and praise. The second stanza asks God to give his Word success—presumably in its preaching. The third stanza speaks of "this glad hour," meaning the hour of Sunday worship. All of these first three stanzas are phrased in terms of supplication, as God is asked to perform certain actions on behalf of believers. Additionally, each of these stanzas begins with a prayer that God will "come." In the fourth stanza, the petitionary mode is replaced by a kind of doxology, which consists of an ascription of praise to God ("eternal praises be"), followed by a wish or desire ("may we . . .").

Kingship is another unifying motif of the poem. The opening line invokes God as an almighty king, and subsequent lines of the stanza ascribe glory, victory, and reigning to God the Father. The second stanza portrays Christ as wearing a mighty sword, in the mode of a conquering warrior-king. The third stanza calls the Holy Spirit "almighty" and ascribes "rule" and "power" to him. The final stanza speaks of God's "sovereign majesty."

The arrangement of the poem around the respective persons of the Trinity leads us to look for distinctive actions of each person of the Trinity, but if we look closely we find that the author worked hard to emphasize what the persons of the Trinity have in common. The motif of power or might, for example, unifies the stanzas (as noted above). All three members of the Godhead are invoked to "come" and dispense spiritual blessing on the company of believers, with the result that the successive stanzas seem cut from the same cloth instead of being differentiated. The second stanza invokes the Son, but the two concluding lines are a transition to the next stanza ("Spirit of holiness, on us descend.").

What looks like a simple poem turns out to be filled with certain ambiguities. We finally ask, Do the persons of the Trinity chiefly differ from each other or share the same identity? In addition, this hymn was originally sung to the same tune as the British national anthem ("God Save the King")—commentators have debated whether it is a harmonious analogy to human kingship or a substitute for it.

A SAMPLING of commentary on this poem quickly shows that it is so filled with biblical allusions that every line can be related to at least one Bible verse. The stanzas of the hymn devoted to individual members of the Trinity reach a climax in the combination of the last stanza, in a manner parallel to the concluding verse of 2 Corinthians:

> The grace of the Lord Jesus Christ and the love of God and the fellowship of the Holy Spirit be with you all. (13:14)

Tell Out, My Soul

Timothy Dudley-Smith (b. 1926)

Tell out, my soul, the greatness of the Lord!
Unnumbered blessings give my spirit voice;
Tender to me the promise of his word;
In God my Savior shall my heart rejoice.

Tell out, my soul, the greatness of his Name!
Make known his might, the deeds his arm has done;
His mercy sure, from age to age the same;
His holy Name—the Lord, the Mighty One.

Tell out, my soul, the greatness of his might!
Powers and dominions lay their glory by;
Proud hearts and stubborn wills are put to flight,
The hungry fed, the humble lifted high.

Tell out, my soul, the glories of his word!
Firm is his promise, and his mercy sure.
Tell out, my soul, the greatness of the Lord
To children's children and for evermore!

T IMOTHY Dudley-Smith, now a retired Anglican bishop, was one of the foremost hymn writers of the second half of the twentieth century. Although he has written some four hundred hymns, this one is both his signature hymn and his first one. A number of themes that undergird this anthology of hymns as poems converge in the original composition of this particular text, so we can profitably take time to explore them. In 1961, Dudley-Smith was reading a review copy of the recently published New English Bible when his attention was captivated by its rendition of the opening line of Mary's Magnificat (her song of praise as she was staying with Elizabeth during the advent account, as found in Luke 1): "Tell out, my soul, the greatness of the Lord." Dudley-Smith "saw in it the first line of a poem, and speedily wrote the rest." The operative word here is *poem*, and the author has explicitly stated that this text was "not written as a hymn." Dudley-Smith became a hymn writer when this poem was solicited as a hymn by the editors of the *Anglican Hymn Book*.

It is entirely possible to experience this poem without knowing that it is an adaptation of Mary's song. In fact, I did not realize this connection until I compiled this anthology, having sung the hymn for many years without that knowledge. Of course, Mary's so-called song was originally a poem, too, not a hymn. We cannot remind ourselves too often that hymns begin as poems.

Whenever we know that a text is modeled on a preexisting text, analyzing what is new and what is indebted to the earlier text is an avenue toward experiencing the poem or hymn. Mary's song is itself modeled on Hannah's song as recorded in 1 Samuel 2:1–10. For purposes of this brief explication, I will explore Dudley-Smith's poem on its own terms.

The first thing to note is that the poem is not specifically a Christmas poem. It would not be classified as a Christmas poem in an anthology of English poetry (and I will note in passing that Dudley-Smith has recorded that scarcely a week goes by without a request for permission to use the hymn at special events such as weddings). The theme of the poem is the same as the theme of psalms of praise in the Psalter—namely, the need to praise God because of his character and acts. In the manner of Psalm 103 ("Bless the Lord, O my soul"), the speaker in the poem commands his own soul to conduct the praise. Every stanza of this poem begins with the conventional command to praise that we find in the genre of the praise psalm.

The remainder of each stanza offers a rationale for the call to praise, and that rationale can also be viewed as the actual content of the praise. The opening stanza is so generalized as to constitute an introduction to the poem. The subject of praise is "the Lord" in total, and the primary subject of this stanza is the speaker's exuberant personal response to God. The three stanzas that follow each have a specific focus of praise: God's name, his might, and his Word. The diction is simple rather than predominantly imagistic, and the poetic effect is achieved by aphoristic phrasing and a certain tightness of syntax (as in "the hungry fed, the humble lifted high").

L UKE 1:46–55 is the text that inspired "Tell Out, My Soul," and Mary's song in its entirety is good collaborative reading. Here is the part of the Magnificat that most directly enters Dudley-Smith's poem:

> He has shown strength with his arm;
> he has scattered the proud in the thoughts of their hearts;
> he has brought down the mighty from their thrones
> and exalted those of humble estate;
> he has filled the hungry with good things,
> and the rich he has sent away empty. (vv. 51–53)

Guide Me, O Thou Great Jehovah

William Williams (1717–1791)

Guide me, O thou great Jehovah,
Pilgrim through this barren land;
I am weak, but thou art mighty;
Hold me with thy powerful hand;
Bread of heaven, bread of heaven,
Feed me till I want no more.

Open now the crystal fountain,
Whence the healing stream doth flow;
Let the fire and cloudy pillar
Lead me all my journey through;
Strong deliverer, strong deliverer,
Be thou still my strength and shield.

When I tread the verge of Jordan,
Bid my anxious fears subside;
Death of death, and hell's destruction,
Land me safe on Canaan's side;
Songs of praises, songs of praises
I will ever give to thee.

Tʜɪs hymn is as much a national hymn of Wales as "Abide with Me" is of England. Its author, William Williams, is considered by some to be the father of Welsh hymnody, as Isaac Watts is of English hymnody. Known informally as the "Welsh Rugby Hymn," this hymn is sung by the crowd at rugby matches in Wales, especially those involving the national rugby team. It has been sung at royal weddings of the Prince of Wales's family, and it was sung at Princess Diana's funeral. Welsh coal miners have sung it while going down to the mines. Martyn Lloyd-Jones considered the author the best hymn writer ever. Originally written in Welsh, this hymnic poem was translated into English in its familiar form by Peter Williams (no relation of the author) in 1771.

For a very good reason, this poem is predictably included in anthologies of the Bible in literature: it is built entirely around biblical material, preeminently the story of the Exodus and the forty-year wandering in the wilderness. Thus we find allusions to manna (the bread from heaven), the pillar of fire that guided the Israelites by night and the pillar of cloud that led them by day, the water that flowed from a rock, the crossing of the Jordan River, and entry into the promised land of Canaan.

But these striking allusions are only the foundation on which further poetic brilliance rests. The allusions are transmuted into metaphors that apply universally, not simply to Old Testament Israel. The wandering through the wilderness becomes the universal pilgrimage through life. The epithet "bread of heaven" refers not only to manna but to Jesus, who declared himself "the true bread from heaven" (John 6:32). The flowing water refers not only to the water miracles of the Exodus but also to the crystal healing stream flowing from God's heavenly throne (see Rev. 22:1–2). The Jordan River is the archetypal river of death, and crossing it leads metaphorically to the Canaan of heaven.

The evocative epithet "death of death" is another poetic triumph. William Williams is almost as well known as a poet as he is a hymn writer, so it is entirely possible that he intended an allusion to the concluding words of John Donne's famous sonnet on immortality: "Death, thou shalt die." Even more likely, Williams, a Calvinistic Methodist, borrowed the words from the title of a Puritan classic: John Owen's *The Death of Death in the Death of Christ.*

The theme of this poem is the power of God to provide for human needs. Based on that premise, the entire poem is a prayer addressed directly to God. Each of the three stanzas includes a reference to God's role as guide on a journey, but the poem is not built around that provision only. There are also references to the archetypal needs of food, drink, deliverance, strength, and companionship at the time of one's death. The speaker in the poem (and we with him) prays from a stance of being weak, needy, and fearful of death. Set over against human weakness are evocative epithets for God: great Jehovah, bread of heaven, strong deliverer, strength and shield, death of death, hell's destruction.

T HIS poem is built on key events of the Old Testament exodus. In a similar manner, Psalm 105 rehearses the events of Old Testament history; the following is an excerpt from that rehearsal.

> He spread a cloud for a covering,
> and fire to give light by night.
> They asked, and he brought quail,
> and gave them bread from heaven in abundance.
> He opened the rock, and water gushed out;
> it flowed through the desert like a river.
> . . . .
>
> So he brought his people out with joy,
> his chosen ones with singing. (vv. 39–41, 43)

100

Be Thou My Vision

Author Unknown (Old Irish; date unknown)

Be thou my vision, O Lord of my heart;
Naught be all else to me, save that thou art.
Thou my best thought, by day or by night,
Waking or sleeping, thy presence my light.

Be thou my wisdom, and thou my true word;
I ever with thee and thou with me, Lord;
Thou my great Father, I thy true son;
Thou in me dwelling, and I with thee one.

Riches I heed not, nor man's empty praise,
Thou mine inheritance, now and always;
Thou and thou only, first in my heart,
High king of heaven, my treasure thou art.

High king of heaven, my victory won;
May I reach heaven's joys, O bright heaven's sun!
Heart of my own heart, whatever befall,
Still be my vision, O ruler of all.

T HE origins of this ancient text are shrouded in mystery, and
the hymn accordingly possesses the fascination of an old

text. The format or genre of the poem is that of a prayer addressed to God. Within this unifying framework of continuous prayer, we find a repeated rhetorical pattern in which the speaker uses the formula "Be thou." It is true that this formula appears verbatim only twice in the "singing" version printed above, but (a) it appears more often in the original text and (b) all the appearances of *thou* in the hymn version are understood to have the command *be* in front of them (as they have in the original). The formula "Be thou" can be viewed as simultaneously *a petition* addressed to God asking him to perform what is expressed, *a command* addressed to the self to make certain that the actions or attitudes that are named occur, and *a wish or desire* that the named situation will be present in the speaker's life. The point of unity in all this rhetorical patterning is the elevation of God to a position of central importance in a believer's life.

The individual stanzas give us variations on the central theme. The first variation focuses on God as a believer's constant *vision*—a word that here encompasses two familiar meanings. A vision is what we *see*, first of all—what is in view and therefore in our attention. Second, a vision is what we are aiming for—the thing that inspires us and guides our actions. Each line in the opening stanza is built around the motif of "God only or supremely."

The unity of the opening stanza gives way to diversity in the second stanza. Each line names a different prayer expressing what the speaker desires God to be in his or her life: wisdom and revelation, a constant companion, a divine parent, and a permanent resident dwelling in the same place as the speaker/reader. The imagery of wealth and treasure occupies the third stanza, as God is declared to be the believer's *riches, inheritance,* and *treasure.*

The final stanza represents the eschatological turn that is common in hymns, as the focus shifts to heaven and the afterlife.

Looked at closely, the final stanza is a summary of what has preceded. God is the bright sun that dominates what we see. The earlier motif of being one with God is repeated with the epithet *heart of my heart*. And the last line repeats the opening request that God be our *vision*, giving the poem an envelope structure. Scattered epithets for God in the first three stanzas now explode into a concentration of them: *high King of heaven, bright heaven's Sun, heart of my own heart, Ruler of all*.

This is a poem about a Christian's priorities. Its strength as a devotional poem is that it puts first things first and subordinates all of life to God.

T HIS hymnic poem makes the bold claim that God needs to be preeminent in our daily lives because he is the greatest treasure. The Christ hymn found in Colossians 1:15–20 similarly asserts the preeminence of Christ. Here is an excerpt from that hymn:

And he is before all things, and in him all things hold together. And he is the head of the body, the church. He is the beginning, the firstborn from the dead, that in everything he might be preeminent. For in him all the fullness of God was pleased to dwell. (vv. 17–19)

A Shelter in the Time of Storm

Vernon J. Charlesworth (1839–1915)

The Lord's our Rock, in him we hide,
A shelter in the time of storm;
Secure whatever ill betide,
A shelter in the time of storm.

A shade by day, defense by night,
A shelter in the time of storm;
No fears alarm, no foes affright,
A shelter in the time of storm.

The raging storms may round us beat,
A shelter in the time of storm;
We'll never leave our safe retreat,
A shelter in the time of storm.

O Rock Divine, O Refuge dear,
A shelter in the time of storm;
Be thou our helper ever near,
A shelter in the time of storm.

Refrain
Oh, Jesus is a Rock in a weary land,
A weary land, a weary land,

Oh, Jesus is a Rock in a weary land,
A shelter in the time of storm.

W RITTEN around 1880, this hymnic poem belongs to what literary scholars call "high Victorianism." The author was a nonconformist (non-Anglican) Baptist minister whose longest tenure of service was as headmaster of Charles Spurgeon's Stockwell Orphanage in London. This orphanage offered shelter, food, clothing, and education to orphans of all religious backgrounds. Although the poem's imagery of shelter is handled in such a way as to make it primarily a nature image, if we place the poem in a context of a home for orphans in one of the world's largest cities of the day, a second level of meaning also emerges. Another context that enriches the hymn is the fact that fishermen on the northern coast of England often sang the song as they approached their harbors in times of sea storms.

The familiar tune to which we sing this hymn was composed by evangelist Ira Sankey, who is associated with the crusades of Dwight L. Moody. Not surprisingly, the title of the tune is "Shelter." The high incidence of repetition might initially mislead us into thinking that the poem does not lend itself to the kind of analysis that this anthology contains. One avenue to seeing the poetic richness and power of the poem is its archetypes.

The three repeated archetypes in this poem emerge as the primary ones: rock, shelter, and storm. The way to assimilate archetypes is to start with our own remembered or current experiences of them. We can ponder the associations of rock, shelter, and storm that have elevated these concepts to such universal stature in the human imagination, starting with their literal, physical properties. Then we can place them and their associations into the broader context of literature as a whole, starting with the Bible.

In addition to these three central archetypes, this poem

secures its effect with image patterns that combine the resources of archetypes and symbols. Images of safe retreat appear in such terms as *hide, shade, defense, retreat,* and *refuge,* with their effect heightened by the accompanying adjectives *secure* and *safe.* Most poems are organized partly around the principle of contrast, and that is part of this poem's strategy as well. Over against the positive archetypes and image patterns discussed thus far are images of hostility that touch us deeply: an all-encompassing *ill* that "betides" (an archaic word for "happens"), *day* with its threatening heat, and *night* with its array of terrors.

Perhaps the crowning stroke of all this poetic richness is the metaphoric *weary land* that haunts the poem. What kind of land is this? Not a physical one, such as a desert. Instead it is an evocative emotional land that we all know but that cannot be plotted on a geographic map. Instead we find this unpleasant land on the map of our minds, emotions, and souls (a spiritual geography).

The large amount of repeated material in this poem initially raises our suspicion that it cannot sustain what literary critics call close reading, but it turns out that there is as much to say about the poetic texture of this poem as there is about other poems in this anthology.

T HIS poem is another case in which finding a parallel passage in the Bible presents us with the proverbial "embarrassment of riches." Nonetheless, Isaiah 4:5–6 rises above its competitors (but see also Isa. 32:2):

> Then the LORD will create over the whole site of Mount Zion and over her assemblies a cloud by day, and smoke and the shining of a flaming fire by night; for over all the glory there will be a canopy. There will be a booth for shade by day from the heat, and for a refuge and a shelter from the storm and rain.

Glorious Things of Thee Are Spoken

John Newton (1725–1807)

Glorious things of thee are spoken,
Zion, city of our God;
He whose word cannot be broken
Formed thee for his own abode;
On the Rock of Ages founded,
What can shake thy sure repose?
With salvation's walls surrounded,
Thou mayest smile at all thy foes.

See the streams of living waters,
Springing from eternal love,
Well supply thy sons and daughters,
And all fear of want remove;
Who can faint, while such a river
Ever flows their thirst to assuage?
Grace which, like the Lord, the giver,
Never fails from age to age.

Round each habitation hovering,
See the cloud and fire appear
For a glory and a covering,
Showing that the Lord is near:

Thus deriving from their banner
Light by night and shade by day,
Safe they feed upon the manna
Which he gives them when they pray.

Savior, if of Zion's city
I, through grace, a member am,
Let the world deride or pity,
I will glory in thy Name;
Fading is the worldling's pleasure,
All his boasted pomp and show;
Solid joys and lasting treasure
None but Zion's children know.

T HIS poem is a meditation on what it means to belong to God's kingdom and family. It is a poem about the believer's citizenship. Mainly the poem catalogs and celebrates the benefits of this citizenship, but in the last stanza the speaker reaches a moment of resolve to persist in loyalty even in the face of ridicule. The poem is as dense with poetic texture (imagery and figurative language) as poems that are taught in college English courses are, but because the poet sticks with biblical archetypes and symbols, the poem meets the hymnic criterion of poetry under vows of renunciation—that is, poetry that is simple enough for the common person to understand and enjoy.

The first great symbol to greet us is Zion, the city of God. In the Bible, Zion is the name given to a literal city and the mountain within it—namely, Jerusalem and the temple mount. It is also a biblical symbol and metaphor for heaven. However, the Zion in Newton's hymn is neither of these but instead a symbol of the company of the redeemed—the spiritual kingdom of God. That having been said, the poem nonetheless attributes to the symbolic city the same qualities that the psalmists ascribed to Jerusalem: it is the abode of God, founded on a stable rock, surrounded by walls, and protected from surrounding enemies. Using the mode of symbolism, the opening stanza thus stresses the stability and security of God's kingdom by picturing it as a secure city.

In stanza 2, the symbolism shifts from the holy city to streams of living water. The energy of the imagery is breathtaking. Feeding into the stanza is a myriad of biblical verses that feature the archetype of flowing water, from either a fountain or a river. From the range of possible symbolic meanings, this stanza distills four aspects of the archetype of flowing water: its abundance, its ability to sustain a person by assuaging thirst, the permanence of its supply, and God as its source. Given this superabundance at our disposal, the poet asks rhetorically, "Who can faint?"

The third stanza whisks us away in our imaginations to the Israelites' journey through the wilderness under God's protection and provision. The specific images that are turned into a metaphoric picture of God's provision and protection in our lives are the pillar of fire by night, the cloud by day, and manna. Newton adds original enriching touches to these images: the cloud and fire hovering over every family's house to show that God is near, a banner that emanates light and shade, and provision that comes specifically to those who pray. All of these metaphors require pondering and unpacking.

The final stanza brings a note of realism into the ecstatic contemplation of the rights of the citizens who belong to Zion. A battle motif enters, with a mention of enemies who deride. The fleetingness of worldly "pomp and show" is contrasted to "solid joys and lasting treasure." This note of realism in no way diminishes the glories of Zion that have been celebrated, but it alerts us that citizenship in God's city requires us to choose it over other options as we realize that citizenship can carry a price tag.

Literary scholar Northrop Frye championed the view that the archetypes and allusions in most works of literature reach outward from a given work to the whole realm of literature, so that "the center of the literary universe is whatever poem we happen to be reading." We can demonstrate this by using a concordance or word search or internet site to guide us to the biblical verses from which Newton composed his poem, taking time to get inside the Bible passages and then reflect on the use that Newton has made of each reference.

T HE point of departure for this poem is Psalm 87:1–3. Although the poem ranges all over the Bible, the opening and closing of Psalm 87 are the best parallel passage:

> On the holy mount stands the city he founded;
>> the LORD loves the gates of Zion
>> more than all the dwelling places of Jacob.
> Glorious things of you are spoken,
>> O city of God.
> . . . .
>
> Singers and dancers alike say,
>> "All my springs are in you." (vv. 1–3, 7)

Jesus Shall Reign

Isaac Watts (1674–1748)

Jesus shall reign where'er the sun
Does his successive journeys run;
His kingdom stretch from shore to shore,
Till moons shall wax and wane no more.

For him shall endless prayer be made,
And praises throng to crown his head;
His name, like sweet perfume, shall rise
With every morning sacrifice.

People and realms of every tongue
Dwell on his love with sweetest song;
And infant voices shall proclaim
Their early blessings on his name.

Blessings abound where'er he reigns;
The prisoner leaps to lose his chains,
The weary find eternal rest,
And all the sons of want are blest.

Let every creature rise and bring
Peculiar honors to our king,

Angels descend with songs again,
And earth repeat the loud Amen.

W E can begin by noting the obvious features of this poem.
Each stanza identifies Jesus in kingly terms, with such words as *reign, kingdom, crown, realms, reigns,* and *king.* Additionally, the first, third, and final stanzas all emphasize the universality of God's rule, and the imagery of this motif is so energetic and emphatic that we just naturally read the intervening two stanzas as also declaring the universality of God's kingship. The poem seems familiar to us because it belongs to a copious genre from the Psalter—namely, the psalm of praise. In this regard, we readily recognize the call or command to praise God ("Let every creature . . ."), the motif of God's universal reign, and the typical psalmic elements (e.g., sun and moon, prayer, morning sacrifice, and infants as well as "every creature" praising God). We feel as though we are reading a psalm.

The context within which we assimilate a poem can influence what we see in it, and this poem illustrates this fact of interpretation particularly well. For starters, Isaac Watts undertook to systematically "Christianize" the Old Testament psalms, and this poem was first published in his volume *Psalms of David, Imitated in the Language of the New Testament.* The effect is similar to Jesus's reading Isaiah 61:1–2 in the synagogue and then announcing, "Today this Scripture has been fulfilled in your hearing" (Luke 4:21). Literary scholars apply the adjective *intertextual* to this situation, meaning that an author is evoking an earlier text in such a way that we are aware of the presence of that text but also realize that something new is being done with it.

The context into which most of us have been conditioned to place this poem is that of a missionary hymn. The element in the poem that enables this interpretation is the word *shall* in the first three stanzas, conveying the thought that Christ's rule will become more and more universal in the world as more and more nations and people are converted.

A third context for this poem is the golden-age visions of apocalyptic and messianic writing in the Bible. These visions portray a coming age of perfection, which is pictured partly metaphorically (e.g., prisoners being released and leaping), partly in generalized images (e.g., blessings abounding), and partly in images of transcendence (e.g., angels descending with shouts). These golden-age prophecies are variously interpreted, and this hymnic poem embodies the same range of meanings (which do not necessarily contradict each other) that scholars ascribe to the biblical visions. The golden age might be (a) a coming millennium of Christ's reign on earth, (b) the blessings of the messianic age that began when Jesus came to earth, and/or (c) the coming blessings of heavenly existence (which are encapsulated in the image of "eternal rest").

This poem possesses a superlative, "all" and "every" quality. It reaches out to encompass as much as possible: *wherever* the sun makes its circuit, *endless* prayer, *every* morning sacrifice, *every* tongue, *every* creature. The cast of characters keeps expanding: people of every tongue, infants, "every creature," angels, and earth. A certain "no stone unturned" quality permeates the poem.

A s part of his project of adding a Christological meaning to Old Testament Psalms, Isaac Watts intentionally paired "Jesus Shall Reign" with Psalm 72. Here are three verses from that psalm:

> May they fear you while the sun endures,
> and as long as the moon, throughout all generations!
> . . . .

May prayer be made for him continually,
and blessings invoked for him all the day!

. . . .

Blessed be his glorious name forever;
may the whole earth be filled with his glory!
Amen and Amen! (vv. 5, 15, 19)

My Hope Is Built on Nothing Less

Edward Mote (1797–1874)

My hope is built on nothing less
Than Jesus' blood and righteousness;
I dare not trust the sweetest frame,
But wholly lean on Jesus' name.

When darkness veils his lovely face,
I rest upon unchanging grace;
In every rough and stormy gale
My anchor holds within the veil.

His oath, his covenant, his blood
Support me in the whelming flood;

When all around my soul gives way,
He then is all my hope and stay.

When I shall launch in worlds unseen,
O may I then be found in him;
Dressed in his righteousness alone,
Faultless to stand before the throne.

Refrain
On Christ, the solid Rock, I stand;
All other ground is sinking sand.

A LONG with a few other selections in this anthology, this hymnic poem is famous to us partly because we sing it to a captivating, foot-tapping melody. Some poems belonging to this category would not have been included here without their musical context. But this is not a mark against them for our purposes; our task is to add an element of literary analysis to a hymn that has already won us on other grounds.

Another thing that this hymnic poem shares with many others in this anthology is that its author was a pastor who composed hymns for his church services. Edward Mote was raised by unbelieving, pub-owning parents in central London. He was converted at age fifteen, was a cabinet maker until the age of fifty-five, and then became a Baptist minister for two decades. On a Sunday when Mote visited a couple in his church who had become shut-ins, the couple informed him about their Sunday routine of singing a hymn and reading from the Bible. Mote thereupon reached into his pocket and retrieved the hymn he had composed while walking to work during the preceding week. The three then sang "My Hope Is Built" for the first time.

Two subjects converge in every stanza of this poem, and when we have noted both of these, we can merge them into a statement of unifying theme. First, every stanza asserts and celebrates the feeling of certainty that the speaker experiences as a Christian. The believer possesses something that is stable, permanent, and reliable. No doubt lurks in the speaker's feeling of being secure. Second, in every stanza the basis of this certainty is declared to be Jesus—specifically his atonement and imputed righteousness (see the last stanza). The theme of the poem is thus the redemptive work of Jesus as the sure foundation of a believer's unwavering hope.

Variations on this central theme consist of changing contexts in which the speaker in the poem trusts in the finished work of Jesus, or various threats to a Christian's certainty. In the opening stanza, the speaker chooses Jesus' blood and righteousness over "the sweetest frame," meaning the most alluring alternative belief system or thing in life that might attract us. The next two stanzas keep the element of contrast alive as an organizing motif, with references to an unidentified spiritual darkness that hides God, the rough and stormy gales of life, a flood, and a comprehensive loss of all human resources that might provide support in the extremities of life ("all around my soul gives way"). The context in which certainty is asserted in the final stanza is the final judgment, and there is a latent element of threat here, too, inasmuch as standing before the judgment throne of God carries the potential of destruction for every person on the basis of deeds "done in the body" (2 Cor. 5:10).

The refrain is a deft touch. It recapitulates the central contrast that we have traced in every stanza between the dependability of Christ's redemptive work and the ultimate unreliability of everything else in life.

T HIS poem alludes to many different parts of the Bible, but Jesus' parable of the wise and foolish house builders is woven throughout the first three stanzas:

> Everyone then who hears these words of mine and does them will be like a wise man who built his house on the rock. And the rain fell, and the floods came, and the winds blew and beat on that house, but it did not fall, because it had been founded on the rock. And everyone who hears these words of mine and does not do them will be like a foolish man who built his house on the sand. And the rain fell, and the floods came, and the winds blew and beat against that house, and it fell, and great was the fall of it. (Matt. 7:24–27)

Savior, Like a Shepherd Lead Us

Dorothy Thrupp (1779–1847)

Savior, like a shepherd lead us,
Much we need thy tender care;
In thy pleasant pastures feed us,
For our use thy folds prepare:
Blessed Jesus, blessed Jesus,
Thou hast bought us, thine we are.

We are thine; do thou befriend us,
Be the guardian of our way;
Keep thy flock, from sin defend us,
Seek us when we go astray:
Blessed Jesus, blessed Jesus,
Hear the children when they pray.

Thou hast promised to receive us,
Poor and sinful though we be;
Thou hast mercy to relieve us,
Grace to cleanse, and power to free:
Blessed Jesus, blessed Jesus,
Let us early turn to thee.

Early let us seek thy favor;
Early let us do thy will;
Blessed Lord and only Savior,
With thy love our bosoms fill
Blessed Jesus, blessed Jesus,
Thou hast loved us, love us still.

T HIS hymnic poem takes as its point of departure one of the central archetypes of the Bible—namely, God as a shepherd who provides for those who follow him. In the New Testament, this archetype becomes slanted more specifically toward Jesus as the Good Shepherd. We should allow the Bible's famous "shepherd passages," such as Psalm 23 and John 10:1–18, to filter into our consciousness as we read and ponder the poem.

The genre and format of the poem are those of a prayer. From start to finish, the speaker addresses his thoughts to Jesus. Nearly every line, moreover, expresses a petition, as the speaker asks Jesus to do something on his or her behalf.

This poem is known as a children's hymn, and since this

label can mislead us, we should analyze the situation before conducting our main exploration of the poem. It is true that the author was a writer of children's poems and hymns. But if it were not for the repeated word *early* and a reference to *children* praying, we would not identify this as a children's poem. The sentiments and theological frame of reference are universal. When this poem is sung as a hymn at services of infant baptism and infant dedication, the infants obviously do not ask on their own behalf to seek God and do his will; these petitions are sung by adults on behalf of the infants. In fact, the logic of the stanzas would be clearer if the formulation were "let *them*" turn to God and seek God's favor and do his will. Furthermore, the motif of seeking God *early* can be interpreted as expressing not chronology or age but a stance of the soul characterized by turning to God as a first recourse, giving him priority immediately as opposed to eventually. Similarly, the reference to the children praying fits right into Jesus' stipulation that we must become as little children to enter the kingdom (Matt. 18:3).

As we look at the text, we see that the image of Jesus as shepherd is present in the first two stanzas only. The epithet *blessed Jesus* appears eight times and functions as a mini-refrain. The first two stanzas are closely modeled on Psalm 23, with the first stanza drawing on the motif of pastures found early in the psalm and the second stanza drawing on the motifs of guidance, protection, and rescue found in the middle of the psalm. The specific focus of the third stanza is acknowledgment of the Savior's salvific acts and power, and on the basis of that the speaker expresses a prayer for himself or herself to turn to Jesus as Savior. The final stanza continues the progression in the poem from specifics to generalities, ending the poem not with pastures and pathways but with petitions to seek God's favor and will and for Jesus' love to fill us.

I will speak personally in saying that by subjecting the hymns

in this anthology to close reading, I have repeatedly been convicted of my vague impressions and inaccurate assumptions
about many of the hymns. The discipline of explication has regularly served as a corrective. In regard to this poem, I now see that
it is not as entirely built around shepherd imagery as the opening
had led me to assume, and additionally that it is not primarily
a children's hymn, though it is appropriate to apply its sentiments to children (as long as we do not think ourselves exempt
as adults).

W HILE this entire poem does draw upon pastoral imagery, most of it draws upon the theology of redemption
in Christ. That is also true of Jesus' Good Shepherd discourse
(John 10:1–18), which is here excerpted:

> I am the door of the sheep. . . . I am the good shepherd. I know
> my own and my own know me, just as the Father knows me
> and I know the Father; and I lay down my life for the sheep.
> (vv. 7, 14–15)

Take My Life, and Let It Be

Frances Ridley Havergal (1836–1879)

Take my life, and let it be
Consecrated, Lord, to thee.
Take my moments and my days;
Let them flow in ceaseless praise.

Take my hands, and let them move
At the impulse of thy love.
Take my feet, and let them be
Swift and beautiful for thee.

Take my voice, and let me sing,
Always, only, for my King.
Take my lips, and let them be
Filled with messages from thee.

Take my silver and my gold;
Not a mite would I withhold;
Take my intellect, and use
Every power as thou shalt choose.

Take my will, and make it thine;
It shall be no longer mine.

Take my heart, it is thine own;
It shall be thy royal throne.

Take my love; my Lord, I pour
At thy feet its treasure store.
Take myself, and I will be
Ever, only, all for thee.

M ODERN poet T. S. Eliot once expressed a fear that writers of devotional poetry face the "danger" (Eliot's term) of writing what they would *like* to feel rather than what they *actually* feel. We are inclined to share Eliot's fear most acutely when poets and hymn writers express extravagant feelings of devotion that exceed what we ourselves have achieved. Surely, we say to ourselves, no one actually feels *that* intensely or selflessly or purely.

Two things can be said to curb our skepticism and potential cynicism. The first is that it is both customary and appropriate for poets to express sentiments that represent an ideal toward which they and we aspire. Love poets, for example, express intensities of romantic passion and devotion to their beloveds that exceed what we regularly feel (with the Song of Solomon being a notable example). Second, when we know enough about an author's life or about the real-life experiences that gave rise to a specific poem, it often turns out that the poem is not fanciful after all.

"Take My Life" can be taken to illustrate both these correctives. The author, Frances Havergal, suffered from ill health nearly all her life and died at the age of forty-two. She herself left an account of this poem's genesis. She was paying a five-day visit to a house with ten people staying in it, all of whom displayed a range of spiritual needs. Frances prayed, "Lord, give me all in this house"—meaning approximately, "Let me be the instrument that brings them to conversion or restores them to the joy of their salvation." God granted her request, and on her last night in the house Frances was too happy to sleep. She renewed her own consecration, and this hymn began to take shape in her imagination. Four years after composing the poem, Havergal was so convicted by her own words about not withholding her silver and gold that she packed and shipped an entire box of valuable jewelry to a church missionary house. In her early years, Frances was a concert hall singer, and later she decided to sing only sacred music, along the lines of "take my voice, and let me sing, always, only, for my King."

The genre of the poem is that of consecration or commitment (and we should note that Frances Havergal is widely known as "the consecration poet," on the basis of this and other poems). The speaker in the poem consecrates or devotes herself wholly to the service of God, becoming a latter-day Abraham, who was commended by God for *not withholding* his only son (see Gen. 22:16). Another genre at work in the poem is that of the prayer addressed directly to God. As the prayer unfolds, it comes to include both petitions addressed to God and promises made by the speaker.

The poem is a triumph of simplicity and symmetry. It consists of twelve parallel sentences, each one a rhymed couplet that begins with the formula "Take my . . ." Further, each couplet has its own subject, so that every stanza consists of two complementary halves. Here is how the inventory of *things offered to God* unfolds, stanza by stanza: life and time; hands and feet; voice and lips; money and intellect; will and heart; love and self. The cumulative effect is part of the poem's genius.

T o consecrate ourselves, our abilities, and our possessions in the manner described in "Take My Life" involves the sacrifice or offering of these things to God. Romans 12:1 commends exactly such sacrifice as an essential ingredient of Christian life and duty:

> I appeal to you therefore, brothers, by the mercies of God, to present your bodies as a living sacrifice, holy and acceptable to God, which is your spiritual worship.

May the Mind of Christ My Savior

Kate B. Wilkinson (1859–1928)

May the mind of Christ my Savior
Live in me from day to day,
By his love and power controlling
All I do and say.

May the word of Christ dwell richly
In my heart from hour to hour,
So that all may see I triumph
Only through his power.

May the peace of Christ my Savior
Rule my life in everything,
That I may be calm to comfort
Sick and sorrowing.

May the love of Jesus fill me,
As the waters fill the sea;
Him exalting, self abasing,
This is victory.

May I run the race before me,
Strong and brave to face the foe,
Looking only unto Jesus
As I onward go.

May his beauty rest upon me
As I seek the lost to win,
And may they forget the channel,
Seeing only him.

T HE most obvious feature of this poem is its repetitive format, in which the speaker (and we with her) lists a series of spiritual acts and qualities using the grammatical construction *may*. What do we intend when we say "may" this or that happen? It is certainly a wish or desire—but in a spiritual context it also carries the force of a prayer. The series of wishes and petitionary prayers in this poem is a declaration or charter of what the speaker and reader aspire to achieve. The effect is a statement of spiritual goals for life—a spiritually minded Christian's wish list.

Rhetorically, the poem is a skillfully composed construct that adheres to what C. S. Lewis in his book *Reflections on the Psalms* calls the basic principle of all art—namely, "the same in the other." In this poem, the element of sameness is that each stanza follows the same rhetorical format, beginning with a grammatical subjunctive statement that starts with the word *may*. Also carried over from stanza to stanza is the naming and elaboration of a specific spiritual virtue for which the speaker longs and prays and commits to.

The element of otherness is that each stanza names and develops a different spiritual virtue. Most of the stanzas take as their point of departure a well known biblical verse. Stanza 1, "May the mind of Christ my Savior," is based on Philippians 2:5: "Let this mind be in you, which was also in Christ Jesus" (KJV). Stanza 2, "May the word of Christ dwell richly in my heart," is an application of the command stated in Colossians 3:16: "Let the word of Christ dwell in you richly." Stanza 3, "May the peace of Christ my Savior rule my life," echoes Colossians 3:15: "Let the peace of Christ rule in your hearts." Stanza 4, "May the love of Jesus fill me," echoes Ephesians 3:19: "[that you may] know the love of Christ . . . [and] be filled with all the fullness of God." Stanza 5, "May I run the race before me," is based on Hebrews 12:1: "and let us run with endurance the race that is set before us." Stanza 6, "May His beauty rest upon me," comes from Psalm 90:17: "And let the beauty of the LORD our God be upon us" (KJV).

This is obviously worked out with great skill, but more remains to ponder. Only the first two lines of each stanza come directly from a specific Bible passage. The remaining two lines represent what the poet decided to do *with* the opening thought taken from the Bible. After we analyze each two-line follow-up in its place in a given stanza, we can put the concluding pairs of lines together and look for unifying patterns. What all these passages have in common is editorialized right in the poem with the line "Him exalting, self abasing." Each of the concluding pairs of lines is built on that two-sided thought.

This poem is a statement of commitment to practice the spiritual virtues that each stanza names and elaborates, but it is also a reality check regarding what we most desire in our lives. At this point we can profitably apply William Wordsworth's theory that a lyric poem can rectify or correct our feelings, along with John Milton's parallel view that a poem sets the affections—the feelings and desires and bent of our wills—in right tune. The sentiments expressed in this poem serve as a curb on our frequent bent toward self-aggrandizement instead of toward being "sold out" to Christ.

O NE reason this poem seems familiar to us is that it is modeled on a format found regularly in the New Testament epistles, in which the author expresses a wish or prayer using the "may" formula. Here is one of those passages:

> To this end we always pray for you, that our God may make you worthy of his calling and may fulfill every resolve for good and every work of faith by his power, so that the name of our Lord Jesus may be glorified in you, and you in him, according to the grace of our God and the Lord Jesus Christ. (2 Thess. 1:11–12)

To God Be the Glory

Fanny J. Crosby (1820–1915)

To God be the glory, great things he hath done;
So loved he the world that he gave us His Son,
Who yielded his life, an atonement for sin,
And opened the life gate, that all may go in.

O perfect redemption, the purchase of blood,
To every believer, the promise of God;
The vilest offender who truly believes,
That moment from Jesus a pardon receives.

Great things he hath taught us, great things he hath done,
And great our rejoicing through Jesus the Son;
But purer, and higher, and greater will be
Our wonder, our transport, when Jesus we see!

Refrain
Praise the Lord, praise the Lord,
Let the earth hear his voice!
Praise the Lord, praise the Lord,
Let the people rejoice!
O come to the Father, through Jesus the Son,
And give him the glory, great things he hath done!

S OMETHING needs to be said first about this poem's author and the history of its reception. Fanny J. Crosby was born near New York City and claimed a strong family Puritan heritage throughout her life. She was blind from the age of six until her death at the age of ninety-five. She wrote more than eight thousand hymns, as well as a thousand poems on other subjects. She was also an activist for numerous causes, including the blind. Although "To God Be the Glory" was composed and published in the United States, it first became famous in Britain through the crusades of Sankey and Moody. It was relatively unknown in the United States until Cliff Barrows began to sing it at Billy Graham crusades in 1954.

The poem taps into something that is at the heart of the Christian faith and has been particularly prominent in the Reformed segment of that faith. First Corinthians 10:31 expresses the principle in kernel form: "So, whether you eat or drink, or whatever you do, do all to the glory of God." The answer to the first question in the Westminster Shorter Catechism is "Man's chief end is to glorify God and to enjoy him forever." Johann Sebastian Bach's signature sign-off on all his religious compositions was the Latin motto *Soli Deo Gloria*: to God alone be the glory. Crosby's famous hymn fits right into this mainstream of Christian experience.

The focus of the poem is specifically the glory that God merits for his redemptive work in Christ. God has done many "great things," but this poem celebrates just one of them. The genre is the poem of praise, which is modeled on the Old Testament psalms of praise. The three stanzas express the actual praise, and the refrain corresponds to the conventional call or command for people to "praise the Lord." There is a second genre at work as well—namely, the gospel call. This comes out most clearly in the concluding two lines of the refrain, with their appeal to "come to" God and give him glory. But the first two stanzas outline the content of the gospel, implicitly appealing to the audience of the hymn and poem to "truly believe" and at "that moment" receive God's pardon.

We can accurately describe the content of the first two stanzas as a primer (a statement of first principles) on the gospel of salvation. The first stanza states the facts about Jesus' substitutionary atonement for sin, thereby rehearsing what God has done in the drama of salvation. The second stanza outlines the condition that sinners must meet in order to claim God's offered redemption—namely, to believe in Jesus as savior.

In the third stanza, the poem takes the familiar eschatological turn of many hymns by shifting our gaze to the consummation of redemption in heaven. The poem treats this as the climax of a reality that is incomplete during our earthly sojourn. The effect is to create a sense of longing to move from the "great" (in the first line of the final stanza) to the "greater" (in the third line).

From start to finish, this poem offers a great antidote to the self-absorption and narcissism of our own culture. It calls us to glorify and praise God, not ourselves.

T HE supreme act of God for which he deserves glory is his plan of redemption. The greatest verse in the Bible encapsulates that act and lies behind Crosby's famous poem:

> For God so loved the world, that he gave his only Son, that whoever believes in him should not perish but have eternal life. (John 3:16)

Christ Is Made the Sure Foundation

John M. Neale (1818–1866)

Christ is made the sure foundation,
Christ the head and cornerstone,
Chosen of the Lord and precious,
Binding all the church in one;
Holy Zion's help forever
And her confidence alone.

All that dedicated city,
Dearly loved of God on high,
In exultant jubilation
Pours perpetual melody;
God the One in Three adoring
In glad hymns eternally.

To this temple, where we call thee,
Come, O Lord of hosts today:
With thy wonted lovingkindness
Hear thy people as they pray;
And thy fullest benediction
Shed within its walls alway.

Here vouchsafe to all thy servants
What they ask of thee to gain,
What they gain from thee forever
With the blessed to retain,
And hereafter in thy glory
Evermore with thee to reign.

Laud and honor to the Father,
Laud and honor to the Son,
Laud and honor to the Spirit,
Ever Three and ever One,
One in might, and One in glory,
While unending ages run.

T HIS poem's author, John M. Neale, is one of the most famous translators of hymns into English. In "Christ Is Made the Sure Foundation," Neale was working with a Latin original from the seventh century, which was allegedly composed for the dedication of a church. Right from the opening line, the poem has a sturdy feel to it. This substantiality of thought and sentiment is embodied in imagery that has an expansive quality that begets confidence as we read or sing the words. This is a poem of exaltation.

The topical outline of the poem shows its progression from stanza to stanza. The first stanza is an exalted declaration of Christ's position in the church. Stanza 2 is similarly declarative, but its focus shifts from Christ as he is in himself to the praise and adoration that the church directs toward him. In stanza 3 the mode shifts from declaration to prayer, as the speaker addresses Christ directly and petitions that he will hear and bless the assembled people. Stanza 4 continues the mode of petitionary prayer, but now the prayer is specifically that Christ will grant his people what they ask from him, now and hereafter in glory. Stanza 5 is a liturgically phrased pronouncement of praise and honor to the triune God throughout the "unending ages" of the eschaton. Literary critics praise the *architectonics* (the superior organizational design) of a well-constructed poem, and this one makes the grade. When we sing a poem such as this one, everything tends to flow together as a single mixture, and we often miss the nuances of progression that the poet built into the poem— nuances that we see when we explicate the text as a poem.

Several image patterns permeate the poem and give it unity. One is architectural imagery suggestive of a city: *foundation, cornerstone, Zion, city, temple, walls.* This holy city, in turn, is a symbol for the company of believers, both on earth and in heaven. A second image pattern is that of unity and "one," expressed in such references as *binding all in one, all that dedicated city,* and the Trinity as *one* (of which there are four occurrences). Third, images of group and assembly are prominent: *church, city,* the *temple* as a gathering place, *thy people, thy servants, the blessed* (with the latter three describing the company of believers).

What literary scholars sometimes call "the search for superlatives" is alive and well in this poem: *all* the church, help *forever,* confidence *alone, exultant* jubilation, *perpetual* melody, glad hymns *eternally, fullest* benediction, shed *always,* gain *forever, unending* ages. Superlative phrases such as these aim to present something in a way that could be described as "not in ordinary or partial measure but in the fullest measure." A final poetic device used prominently in this poem is allusion—the poet seems to have a single main allusion in mind (along with numerous secondary ones) in each respective stanza, as follows: in stanza 1, Christ as cornerstone (Eph. 2:20–22, buttressed by 1 Peter 2:4–8); in stanza 2, Zion as a dedicated city (Ps. 48); in stanzas 3 and 4, Solomon's prayer for God to hear his people (2 Chron. 6:12–42); in stanza 5, the Trinitarian formula (Matt. 28:19).

A s already noted, this poem evokes many Bible passages. The opening of the poem is so famous, and the hymn itself so closely associated with it, that Ephesians 2:19–21 seems inevitable as a parallel passage:

> The household of God [is] built on the foundation of the apostles and prophets, Christ Jesus himself being the cornerstone, in whom the whole structure, being joined together, grows into a holy temple in the Lord. In him you also are being built together into a dwelling place for God by the Spirit.

God Moves in a Mysterious Way

William Cowper (1731–1800)

God moves in a mysterious way
His wonders to perform;
He plants his footsteps in the sea,
And rides upon the storm.

Deep in unfathomable mines
Of never-failing skill
He treasures up his bright designs,
And works his sovereign will.

Ye fearful saints, fresh courage take;
The clouds ye so much dread
Are big with mercy, and shall break
In blessings on your head.

Judge not the Lord by feeble sense,
But trust him for his grace;
Behind a frowning providence
He hides a smiling face.

His purposes will ripen fast,
Unfolding every hour;

The bud may have a bitter taste,
But sweet will be the flower.

Blind unbelief is sure to err,
And scan his work in vain.
God is his own interpreter,
And he will make it plain.

W ILLIAM Cowper is a well-known English poet whose career as a hymn writer was part of a larger literary life. Cowper led an emotionally troubled life and suffered from severe bouts of depression, resulting in multiple suicide attempts. He came to reside in the town of Olney, where John Newton was pastor. Newton was a great blessing to Cowper, and the two of them collaborated on a collection of original hymns entitled *Olney Hymns* (1779). "God Moves in a Mysterious Way" was the last hymn that Cowper composed, either just before or after an attempt at suicide by drowning. When it appeared in the *Olney Hymns* book, it bore the title "Light Shining Out of Darkness."

There is more going on in this poem than we might initially think. The obvious theme of the poem is divine providence. As Cowper turns that prism in the light, we are led to contemplate various aspects of God's providence, and taking the time to name these is a good avenue toward assimilating the poem. A loose outline is the following (but it should not be allowed to deter us from finding more specific angles of vision within the broad outline): stanzas 1 and 2 assert that God's "ways" and "designs" (code words for providence) are mysterious to human understanding; stanzas 3 and 4 both begin with direct commands regarding providence ("take courage"; "judge not"; "trust"), which are then supported by reasons to heed the commands; stanzas 5 and 6 elaborate the consolation motif that is latent in stanzas 1–4. The poem is built on a principle of incremental (growing) repetition, as the cumulative weight of assertions about God's benevolence in hostile circumstances keeps getting stronger in our thinking and feeling.

The mystery of God's benevolent providence in human lives is the theme in the foreground. As we continue to ponder the stanzas, certain other topics place themselves on our agenda of meditation as well. One is the portrait of God that emerges. It is a many-sided portrait that includes a strong sense of God's transcendence (as he is declared to be above human understanding), sovereignty (as he controls events and directs their outcomes), and benevolence (as the poem repeatedly claims that the ultimate outcome of seemingly bad circumstances is something good). Then, as an additional overlay, the poem paints a pessimistic picture of human life in a fallen world, which spares the strong claims that everything will be good from seeming glib.

Thus we have the convergence of a picture of God, a picture of human life in extremity, and a background chorus of consolation assuring us that "all shall be well, and all manner of thing shall be well." By now it is apparent that Cowper's poem belongs to the branch of philosophy known as theodicy, which reconciles (a) the sovereignty of God and (b) the benevolence of God toward people with (c) the fact of suffering in the world.

The foregoing richness of content comes to us through a relatively complex poetic texture, as we would expect from a major poet. Thus we find an allusion to psalms, in which God is pictured as walking on the sea and riding the clouds (stanza 1), a metaphor of God's designs being mines of ore in the earth (stanza 2), and a metaphor of bad events in our lives being bitter buds that need to ripen before they taste good (stanza 5). In stanza 3, the poet inverts the conventional meaning of a negative image, as big clouds that break on our heads turn out to be conveyers of mercy.

C OWPER'S poem expresses sentiments that are so contrary to what we sometimes experience and feel that we can accept them only by an act of extreme faith. Two verses from Romans were perhaps in Cowper's mind as he composed his poem:

> And we know that for those who love God all things work together for good. (8:28)

> Oh, the depth of the riches and wisdom and knowledge of God! How unsearchable are his judgments and how inscrutable his ways! (11:33)

Fill Thou My Life, O Lord My God

Horatius Bonar (1808–1889)

Fill thou my life, O Lord my God,
In every part with praise,
That my whole being may proclaim
Thy being and thy ways.

Not for the lip of praise alone,
Nor even the praising heart,
I ask, but for a life made up
Of praise in every part;

Praise in the common things of life,
Its goings out and in,
Praise in each duty and each deed,
However small and mean.

Fill every part of me with praise;
Let all my being speak
Of thee and of thy love, O Lord,
Poor though I be, and weak.

So shall no part of day or night
From sacredness be free:
But all my life, in every step,
Be fellowship with thee.

T HE significance of this hymnic poem will emerge if we place it in a Puritan context. The author was a belated Puritan, a minister in the Church of Scotland who viewed himself as a kindred spirit with two other famous Scottish ministers of his day: Thomas Chalmers and Robert Murray McCheyne. "Fill Thou My Life, O Lord My God" expresses a Puritan and Reformed view of what it means to espouse a sacramental view of life. In liturgical or "high church" circles, the sacramental vision entails multiplying ritual and visible images within a church building. "Sacred space" becomes church interiors that are set apart from everyday life. The Puritan sacramental vision is based on the opposite premise of making all of life sacred by bringing God and spiritual reality into the common life. A typical Puritan statement is that a person who lives with God at the center of his life will find that "his shop as well as his chapel is holy ground."

This is the message of "Fill Thou My Life," which is cast into the form of a prayer addressed to God. The opening stanza is a grand introduction to everything that follows. It is a single sweeping sentence in which the speaker addresses God in a stance of prayer ("O Lord my God"), states a petition ("Fill thou my life"), and offers a reason for the petition ("That my whole being may proclaim . . ."). These three ingredients will govern the entire poem: addresses to God, petitions, and reasons for the petitions.

This poem is built on the classic three-part structure of most lyric poems. Following the introduction, the middle three stanzas develop the main theme of asking for God's infilling. The desired result of this infusion of divine presence is the ability to praise God (with the word *praise* appearing six times in these three stanzas).

The concluding stanza ends the poem on a note of closure by stating a resulting consequence, as signaled by the transition *so* (meaning "thus" or "as a consequence"). The line of argument is this: if God will fill the speaker's life to enable him or her to praise God fully, then "no part of day or night from sacredness [shall] be free." The poet's image of God's fellowship "in every step" echoes a Puritan statement that when a person performs daily work to honor God, "then every step and stroke in your trade is sanctified."

Word patterns count for a lot in this poem. The most notable are the following: *fill* (twice), *whole*, *every* (four times), *all* (twice), and *each* (twice). These associations of super-abundance are supplemented by statements of the arena within which God's infilling to occur: *my life, a life,* and *my life*—which are implied to contrast to just a limited sphere of daily living. The following word pattern rounds out the picture by naming the actions that the speaker will perform with God's infilling: *praise* (seven times), *proclaim,* and *speak.*

T HIS poem expresses an ideal in which no part of life is exempt from sacredness. Zechariah 14:20–21 paints a similar picture of life in which even the most common things are holy:

> And on that day there shall be inscribed on the bells of the horses, "Holy to the LORD." And the pots in the house of the LORD shall be as the bowls before the altar. And every pot in Jerusalem and Judah shall be holy to the LORD of hosts.

Jesus, the Very Thought of Thee

Bernard of Clairvaux (1090–1153)

Jesus, the very thought of thee
With sweetness fills my breast;
But sweeter far thy face to see,
And in thy presence rest.

Nor voice can sing, nor heart can frame,
Nor can the memory find,
A sweeter sound than thy blest Name,
O Savior of mankind.

O hope of every contrite heart,
O joy of all the meek,

To those who fall, how kind thou art!
How good to those who seek!

But what to those who find? Ah, this
Nor tongue nor pen can show;
The love of Jesus, what it is
None but his loved ones know.

Jesus, our only joy be thou,
As thou our prize wilt be;
Jesus, be thou our glory now,
And through eternity.

T HIS poem by the medieval French monk Bernard of
Clairvaux is a meditation on the supreme value that
Jesus represents to the believing soul. The poem epitomizes
the mystical temperament of the author (which is also captured in another poem in this anthology by Bernard: "Jesus,
Thou Joy of Loving of Hearts"). The translator of the hymn as
printed above is the British Catholic Edward Caswall (1814–
1878), who is best known for his translations of Catholic Latin
hymns into English.

The genre is the prayer of personal devotion. To begin with
a direct address to Jesus as this poem does is a hymnic convention. It is a truism that while lyric poems are by definition
the expression of the personal feeling or reflection of the poet,
a distinction exists between lyrics that seem directed to us as
readers (e.g., "O Worship the King") and those in which the
poet turns his back on us, leading us to overhear him. "Jesus, the
Very Thought of Thee" is an overheard meditation. It is easy to
imagine Bernard sitting in a monastery garden at his morning
devotions, contemplating what Jesus means to him.

The poem has an envelope structure in which the opening and closing stanzas strike a similar note of outpouring to Jesus as the object of highest devotion. Both stanzas begin with a direct address to Jesus. Within this structure there is also progression, as the final stanza contains the only petitions in the poem. In every stanza the poem evokes longing for Jesus. The middle three stanzas employ a repetitive structure by asserting the supreme worth of Jesus from various angles.

One of Bernard's strategies is to create a ladder in which the good progresses into something even better—namely, the best. In the opening stanza, for example, the *thought* of Jesus fills the breast with sweetness, but it is *sweeter far* to see Jesus. As we read stanza 3, with its celebration of Jesus as the object of human hope and joy, along with its declaration of "how good" Jesus is to those who seek him, we are left feeling that seeking him is the ultimate ideal. But then stanza 4 springs a surprise on us by asserting that "those who find" Jesus achieve something even better than those who seek him.

Bernard also skillfully manages to find a myriad of ways to create the impression that Jesus is the ultimate treasure. *The very thought* of Jesus—just thinking about him—*fills* the breast. In stanza 2, nothing imaginable is *sweeter* than Jesus' blest name. In stanza 3, Jesus is said to be the hope of *every* contrite heart and *all* the meek. In stanza 4, *no* tongue or pen can show what the love of Jesus is. And in the concluding stanza, the speaker prays that Jesus will be our *only* joy (that is, our supreme joy). This poem has a flavor all its own.

A final triumph of the poem is its awakening of spiritual longing. As the prism of Jesus' superiority turns in the light, we progressively long to claim this highest prize. The poem uses conceptual imagery (words that name abstractions rather than sensory images) to awaken our deepest desires: *sweetness, hope, joy, kindness, love, glory*.

T HIS poem evokes a picture of Jesus as the object of our greatest longing and valuing—the one who is above anything else. This is where the speaker of Psalm 73 also landed after having nearly lost his faith when he envied the prosperous wicked:

> Whom have I in heaven but you?
>> And there is nothing on earth that I desire besides you.
> My flesh and my heart may fail,
>> But God is the strength of my heart and my portion forever. (vv. 25–26)

Praise to the Lord, the Almighty

Joachim Neander (1650–1680)

Praise to the Lord, the Almighty, the king of creation!
O my soul, praise him, for he is thy health and salvation!
All ye who hear,
Now to his temple draw near,
Join me in glad adoration.

Praise to the Lord, who o'er all things so wondrously reigneth,
Shelters thee under his wings, yea, so gently sustaineth!
Hast thou not seen

How thy desires e'er have been
Granted in what he ordaineth?

Praise to the Lord, who doth prosper thy work and defend thee!
Surely his goodness and mercy here daily attend thee;
Ponder anew
What the Almighty will do,
If with his love he befriend thee!

Praise thou the Lord, who with marvelous wisdom hath made
thee,
Decked thee with health, and with loving hand guided and
stayed thee.
How oft in grief
Hath not he brought thee relief,
Spreading his wings to o'ershade thee!

Praise to the Lord! O let all that is in me adore him!
All that hath life and breath, come now with praises before him.
Let the Amen
Sound from his people again;
Gladly for aye we adore him.

T HIS poem was composed by a German schoolteacher
when he was a young man in his twenties (he later died
at the age of thirty). Two centuries later, it was translated into
English by Catherine Winkworth, one of the most prolific translators in English hymnody and the most important conduit of
German hymns into English.

The genre is the poem of praise to God, which is closely modeled on the biblical psalms of praise. Such psalms are comprised
of the following stock ingredients: a formal call or command
to praise God, a naming of the person or group to whom the

exhortation is directed, a list or catalog of God's praiseworthy actions, and a note of closure and finality to end the poem. The length of the first two lines of each stanza in this hymn, which are twice the length of the following lines, is one of the elements that lifts this praise psalm into the genre of the ode—an exalted lyric poem written in a high style on a momentous subject.

The opening call to praise in stanza 1 immediately elevates us. The first line consists of three successive epithets for God. The first person addressed is the speaker's own soul, in a move doubtless influenced by Psalm 103:1, which reads, "Bless the LORD, O my soul, and all that is within me, bless his holy name!" Once this note of self-exhortation is introduced, we just naturally read the rest of the poem as being addressed to ourselves. But the rest of the opening stanza quickly broadens the scope by calling the whole company of believers to join in the speaker's personal act of praise. So the effect of poem is double, as we take stock of God's acts in our personal lives but also exhort others to do the same regarding their lives.

The middle three stanzas express the actual praise. The list of praiseworthy acts does not follow a stanza-by-stanza pattern but is a mingled web. God is continually implied to be sovereign in his providence, as he is described as reigning, sustaining, ordaining, defending, directing, and such like. The dominant category of this divine providence is not cosmic but personal and comforting, as God shelters under his wings, grants personal desires, daily attends, befriends, gives health, comforts in grief, and so on. This is a poem not about redemption but about divine presence in earthly and human life. God is shown to be strong on behalf of those who trust him. The overall effect of these stanzas is to get us to look back over God's presence in our lives to the present moment.

The concluding stanza circles back to the opening stanza. Again the poet evokes Psalm 103 by exhorting "all that is in me."

Again the whole company of believers is exhorted to join the praise, as the opening "all ye who hear" now becomes "all that hath life and breath." There is a hint of the conventional eschatological turn in the last line, with its picture of adoring God "for aye"—that is, eternally.

A feature of most of the poems in this anthology is that the poets refer to many passages in the Bible in order to form the poetic texture of each poem. The following list identifies only the passages that are most obviously tied to this poem: references to God's protecting wings draw from Psalm 91:4 and Matthew 23:37; the reference to God's prospering the work of our hands draws from Psalm 90:17; and the reference to "all that hath life and breath" draws from Psalm 150:6.

T HIS poem paints a picture of God's benevolent presence in our lives at every moment of need. Zephaniah 3:17–18 paints an identical picture:

> The LORD your God is in your midst,
>> a mighty one who will save;
> he will rejoice over you with gladness;
>> he will quiet you by his love;
> he will exult over you with loud singing.
>> I will gather those of you who mourn for the festival.

Conclusion

T HE first thing that a reader should do upon finishing a
book is to take stock of what has happened during the
reading of the book. This is both retrospective, as we look back
over the reading experience, and introspective, as we ponder
what changes or clarification might have occurred within us
while we were reading and assimilating the book. Surely most
readers of this book will have been given a new and different
experience of the hymns. Even to see them printed as poems
can be a small revolution in how we assimilate hymnic poems.
In addition, we can now see that all the usual elements of poetry
are present in these texts.

Having taken stock of our reading of this book and its
impact, we should remember that (as T. S. Eliot said in his poem
"Little Gidding") "to make an end is to make a beginning." What
is the takeaway from this book? An obvious answer is that we
can use this book as Christians used words-only hymnbooks
before 1870, incorporating it into our daily devotions, enjoying
it as part of our free-time reading, and using it as an anthology of
devotional poetry. We can also nurture our awareness that hymns
are poems; the explications of the poems in this anthology are a
model of how we can do this. The appearance of hymnic poems
in our conventional hymnbooks is an obstacle to experiencing them as poems—fortunately, the internet is a ready source
for seeing the hymn texts printed as poetry. A hymn website

such as *Hymnary.org* or *The Cyber Hymnal* (www.hymntime
.com) can become an online anthology of hymnic poems—one
that is free for the taking.

For literati who love devotional poetry by such poets as John
Donne, George Herbert, and John Milton, there is a complementary lesson to be learned and a reading habit to be formed.
You, too, have had your eyes opened to something new—namely,
that hymns are not second-rate poetry to be mentioned but not
studied in literature courses. The best poetic hymns hold up
under the same type of explication that English and American
poetry does. And since hymnic poems represent poetry under
vows of renunciation—that is, with the impulse toward complexity and difficulty curbed—they make an excellent initiation
into poetry for the common reader. That is a mark in their favor.
After all, the Bible, including its poetry, is a book of the people.

If I might be allowed a personal note in my role as author,
I have been a professor of English for over half a century, and
this book has been a revelation to me, too. I knew only vaguely
that hymns are poems. I did not realize what a transformation
occurs when we see hymns printed as sequential poems unac-
companied by music. Composing this book became the most
enjoyable of my more than fifty books, as I applied my usual
methods of explication to an unexplored body of literature.
I wish someone had taken me by the hand at the beginning of
my career and said, "Look."

Notes

11 On the format of hymnals before 1870: Christopher N. Phillips, prologue to *The Hymnal: A Reading History* (Baltimore: Johns Hopkins University Press, 2018). The book's subtitle shows its link to *40 Favorite Hymns on the Christian Life*, as the author traces the history of hymns as poems that were *read* rather than sung.

22 A biographer claims: Jonathan Aitken, *John Newton: From Disgrace to Amazing Grace* (Wheaton, IL: Crossway, 2007), 224.

29 On archetypes: A reference book that compiles all the archetypes of the Bible and then subjects them to analysis is a thousand-page book entitled *Dictionary of Biblical Imagery*, ed. Leland Ryken, James C. Wilhoit, and Tremper Longman III (Downers Grove, IL: InterVarsity Press, 1998).

29 Ralph Waldo Emerson claimed: See his essay "The Poet," in *Major Writers of America*, ed. Perry Miller (New York: Harcourt, Brace, and World, 1962), 1:531.

33 A website called *Congregational Singing*: "The Church's One Foundation," Congregational Singing, accessed October 2, 2018, http://www.congsing.org/the_churchs_one.html. This website lists marginal Scripture references for all the hymns on which it posts commentary.

42 On Wesley's reading of Martin Luther: See John R. Tyson, *Assist Me to Proclaim: The Life and Hymns of Charles Wesley* (Grand Rapids: Eerdmans, 2007), 49.

56 A stylistic trait called "the vocative O": Some seventy-five hymns listed in the index of *The Trinity Hymnal* begin with the vocative "O."

58 A summons to "come": The *Trinity Hymnal* contains two dozen hymns that begin with the command or petition to "come."

75 A 2013 poll: "The UK's Top 100 Hymns," BBC One, accessed September 27, 2018, http://www.bbc.co.uk/programmes /articles/3DnJQz7zsF1JrB3rZ8yQ86w/the-uks-top-100-hymns.

79 "to rectify [people's] feelings": William Wordsworth, "Of the Principles of Poetry and His Own Poems," in *The Prose Works of William Wordsworth*, vol. 2, *Aesthetical and Literary*, ed. Alexander B. Grosart (London, 1876), 211.

85 A literary scholar . . . on Baxter: N. H. Keeble, *Richard Baxter: Puritan Man of Letters* (Oxford: Oxford University Press, 1982).

86 Quotes from Milton's sonnet on blindness: John Milton, "Sonnet XVI," in *Poems, &c. Upon Several Occasions* (London, 1673), 59.

90 Lewis famously said: See his essay "The Literary Impact of the Authorised Version," in C. S. Lewis, *Selected Literary Essays*, ed. Walter Hooper (Cambridge: Cambridge University Press, 1969), 133.

96 "saw in it the first line" and "not written as a hymn": Timothy Dudley-Smith, *Lift Every Heart: Collected Hymns 1961–1983 and Some Early Poems* (Carol Stream, IL: Hope Publishing Company, 1984), 12–13.

96–97 Dudley-Smith has recorded: Dudley-Smith, *Lift Every Heart*, 260.

99 Martyn Lloyd-Jones considered: See "William Williams and Welsh Calvinistic Methodism," in *The Puritans: Their Origins and Successors*, ed. D. M. Lloyd-Jones (Edinburgh: Banner of Truth Trust, 1987), 192.

100 "Death, thou shalt die": "Sonnet X," in the Holy Sonnets, first published in John Donne, *Poems* (London, 1633). The poem is also known by its opening words, "Death, be not proud."

110 "the center of the literary universe": Northrop Frye, *Anatomy of*

Criticism: Four Essays (Princeton: Princeton University Press, 1957), 121.

122 "danger": T. S. Eliot, *George Herbert* (London: Longmans, Green, and Company, 1962), 24. An excerpt of the book that includes this quotation is available online at http://web .archive.org/web/20030704062614/http:/www.geocities.com /magdamun/herberteliot.html.

122–23 On the origin of Havergal's poem: The author's autobiographical account can be found in Maria Vernon Graham Havergal, *Memorials of Frances Ridley Havergal* (London: James Nesbet, 1881), 132–33.

125 "the same in the other": C. S. Lewis, *Reflections on the Psalms* (New York: Harcourt, Brace, and World, 1958), 4.

126 William Wordsworth's theory: See Wordsworth, *The Prose Works*, 2:211.

126–27 John Milton's parallel view: See his essay "The Reason of Church Government Urged against Prelaty," in *The Complete Poetical Works of John Milton*, ed. Douglas Bush (Boston: Houghton Mifflin, 1965), xxix.

136 "all shall be well": Julian of Norwich, "The Thirteenth Revelation," in *Revelations of Divine Love*; later quoted by T. S. Eliot in his poem "Little Gidding" in *Four Quartets* (New York: Harcourt, 1943).

138 "his shop as well as his chapel": George Swinnock, *The Christian Man's Calling*, vol. 1, chap. 4 (1662), quoted in Richard B. Schlatter, *The Social Ideas of Religious Leaders, 1660–1688* (1940; repr., New York: Octagon Books, 1971), 189.

139 "then every step and stroke": Richard Steele, *The Tradesman's Calling* (London, 1684), 92.

141 To begin with a direct address to Jesus: In fact, some twenty hymns in *The Trinity Hymnal* begin with the direct address "Jesus, . . ."

147 "To make an end": T. S. Eliot, "Little Gidding," *Four Quartets*.

Glossary of Literary Terms

Allusion. A reference to an event from past history or to a written text from the past. Hymns are filled with allusions to the Bible.

Aphorism. A concise, memorable statement. The Bible is the most aphoristic book in the world, and the classic hymns included in this anthology are likewise a never-failing fountain of beautiful aphorisms. An aphorism is an example of verbal beauty, and a leading function of poetry is the creation of verbal beauty.

Apostrophe. A figure of speech in which a speaker directly addresses a person or thing that is not literally present as though it were present and capable of responding. For example, the final stanza of "O for a Thousand Tongues" is built entirely out of apostrophes, starting with, "Hear him, ye deaf."

Archetype. An image or symbol (such as a river), plot motif (such as a journey), or character type (such as a shepherd) that recurs throughout literature and life. Archetypes are the components of universal human experience and the main building blocks of literature. They evoke powerful elemental and primal feelings in us. The Bible is our primary storehouse of these master images.

Doxology. A poem built around the motif of a call or command to praise God.

153

Elegy. A funeral poem. Its adjectival form is *elegiac*, which is sometimes used broadly to mean "sad."

Epithet. A title for a person or thing. Epithets are a feature of the high style, elevating a statement above everyday discourse. To call God "the ancient of days" is an epithet.

Eschatological turn. The common strategy of hymn writers to shift the focus in a hymn's final stanza to the last things or to life in heaven. Half of the hymns in this anthology take an eschatological turn in their last stanzas.

Explication. A close reading or analysis of a literary text, especially a poem.

Hymnic poem. A poem that is also a hymn to be sung. The word *poem* indicates that the text (a) started as a poem without accompanying music and (b) has all the qualities of a poem. The adjective *hymnic* indicates that the poem is also a hymn that is sung to music. Hymnic poems are also poetry vows of renunciation—for more on that subject, see the glossary entry for *vows of renunciation*.

Image. Any word naming a thing or action. The image is the basic building block of poetry. Poets think in images, and readers need to do the same.

Imagery. A word that names either the entire collection of images in a poem or a pattern of images in a poem. In "Rock of Ages," the imagery of the rock pervades the poem.

Intertextual. Used of a work of literature that refers so conspicuously to an earlier text that our attention is fixed on the interaction between the two texts. We cannot read the later text without also thinking about the earlier one. For instance, Richard Baxter's hymn "Ye Holy Angels Bright" makes such obvious use of the strategy found in Psalm 148—an ever-changing list of apostrophes to various entities—that we cannot assimilate it without thinking of Psalm 148.

Lyric poem; lyric. A short poem expressing the thoughts and feelings of a speaker in his or her own voice (as opposed to being projected onto external characters, the way a story does). Stylistic features of lyrics include a strong sense of unity, careful organization, attention to progression of thought or feeling, packaging of the content in stanzas with rhyming lines, embodiment of meaning in the standard poetic idiom of images and figures of speech, verbal beauty, a maximum of artistry, concentration or compression of thought and feeling. All of the hymnic poems in this anthology are lyric poems. It is appropriate to think of a lyric poem as a performance in words and to regard the poet's skill as a display of craft and artistic beauty that is harnessed in the service of the poem's content. Few of the poems in this anthology were written by people who thought of themselves as poets, yet the eloquence and verbal beauty of their poems are plain to see. A divine benediction has fallen on their compositions.

Metaphor. An implied comparison between two things that does not use the explicit formula *like* or *as*. "A mighty fortress is our God" is a metaphor.

Ode. An exalted poem written in a high style on an exalted subject. We should picture poems as existing on a stylistic continuum, with simplicity dominating on one end and exaltation and high style on the other. The more that a poem moves toward the exalted end of the continuum, the more natural it becomes to call it an ode.

Rhetoric; rhetorical. Throughout the centuries, *rhetoric* has meant two complementary things: (1) strategies of persuasion; (2) a set of stylistic techniques that stand out as being artistic or eloquent, such as repeated words or phrases, question and answer constructions, or a series of sentences or clauses that follow the same pattern (such as "when" clauses followed by "then" clauses, in the successive stanzas of "How Great Thou Art").

Rhetorical question. A question whose answer is obvious. The intention, therefore, is not to elicit information but to lead the reader to assent and register agreement. When the hymn writer asks, "What more can he [God] say than to you he hath said?" we are moved to agree with the writer—God cannot say anything more than the promises he has already made in the Bible.

Simile. A comparison that uses the explicit formula *like* or *as*. "Like a river glorious is God's perfect peace" is a simile.

Vocative O. A direct address to someone using the exclamation "O" as the lead-in. "O Worship the King" uses the vocative O. This rhetorical formula expresses a sense of the momentousness of the subject and occasion, and because it is an exclamation, it conveys excitement as well.

Vows of renunciation. A phrase commonly attributed to hymns as a form of poetry, which makes metaphoric use of the custom of monks and nuns to adopt an ascetic form of life. Writers of hymns write a simple form of poetry that does not use the more complex or difficult devices that mainstream poetry employs. Hymnic poetry is accessible to a broader range of the public than poetry taught in college literature courses. It is great poetry, but simplified poetry in which the poet has limited or curbed the available resources of poetry.

More from P&R Publishing

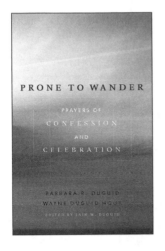 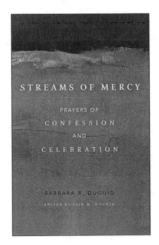

Confessing our sins might seem like a gloomy business . . . but exposing the specifics of our struggles with sin leads to celebration! It points us back to the good news of the gospel, our great Savior, and our forgiveness through God's grace.

Inspired by the Puritan classic *The Valley of Vision*, the prayers in these two volumes are ideal for use in church services or personal devotions. They open with a scriptural call of confession, confess specific sins, thank the Father for Jesus' perfect life and death in our place, ask for the help of the Spirit in pursuing holiness, and close with an assurance of pardon.

"[*Prone to Wander*] has many virtues. . . . The book covers the whole of the Christian life. I love its overall aims and method."
—Leland Ryken

"Here we learn how to pray God's Word back to him . . . and celebrate his grace in so many areas of our lives. I recommend [*Streams of Mercy*] strongly."
—John Frame

More from P&R Publishing

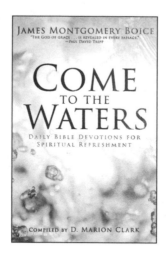

"Study of the Bible must be the consuming passion of a believer's life."

This yearlong devotional selects from the fruit of James Montgomery Boice's labor, distilling his teaching into daily readings that take you from Genesis to Revelation and lead you every day to Jesus Christ, the life-giving Living Water for your soul.

"Read and savor. These devotionals will cause you to love not only the Word of God but, more importantly, the God of grace who is revealed in every passage."
—Paul David Tripp

"James Montgomery Boice was . . . one of the most gifted preachers of our age. Here is the best of Boice in one volume, a compilation of his many preaching gems."
—Steven J. Lawson